Couchsurfing in Iran

COUCHSURFING IN IRAN

REVEALING A HIDDEN WORLD

STEPHAN ORTH

GREYSTONE BOOKS

Vancouver/Berkeley

The translation of this work was supported by a grant from the Goethe-Institut, which is funded by the German Ministry of Foreign Affairs.

18 19 20 21 22   5 4 3 2 1

Greystone Books Ltd.
www.greystonebooks.com

Cataloguing data available from Library and Archives Canada
ISBN 978-1-77164-280-4 (pbk.)
ISBN 978-1-77164-281-1 (epub)

Copy editing by Jennifer D. Foster
Proofreading by Shirarose Wilensky
Cover design by Peter Cocking
Interior design by Nayeli Jimenez
Photo credits:
Stephan Orth (insert, pages 4, 5, 8 below, 9, 12–14, 17–21, 22 below, 23; text, all except page 102)
Mina Esfandiari (insert, pages 1, 2, 3, 6, 7, 8 top, 10, 11, 22 top, 24; text, page 102)
Samuel Zunder (insert, pages 15, 16)
Map credit: Brigit Kohlhaas

Printed and bound in Canada on ancient-forest-friendly paper by Friesens.

Every attempt has been made to trace ownership of copyrighted material. Information that will allow the publisher to rectify any credit or reference is welcome.

We gratefully acknowledge the support of the Canada Council for the Arts, the British Columbia Arts Council, the Province of British Columbia through the Book Publishing Tax Credit, and the Government of Canada for our publishing activities.

TABLE OF CONTENTS

At the border 1

Welcome to Iran! 6

Down with the U.S. 15

Long live the shah 23

Couchsurfing for beginners 29

Torture 33

Freedom 41

The Persian Gulf 52

Lost in transportation I 60

Aryans 64

The genie 69

Lost in transportation II 74

Earthquakes 82

Art 87

The desert 93

Bureaucracy 100

Fake marriage 105

Lost in transportation III 114

Hide-and-seek 117

Poetry 123

Hiking 129

The red Persian carpet   133
Nuclear power   136
Lost in transportation IV   144
War   150
Backgammon   161
Music   168
Smugglers   171
The police   176
The prince   183
Love   187
News   197
A river without water   200
Dictatorship   207
Drunk to the imam   215
Religion and money   219
Party   223
Lost in visa application   227
Green, white, red   234
Fun   238
Orwell   243
Life's caravan   250
Country of surprises   256
Happy ending   261

Acknowledgments   266
Notes   268

62 days in Iran

22 hosts

Total miles traveled (including day trips): 5,271

BY PLANE: 1,413

BY SHIP: 53

BY ROAD: 3,805

AT THE BORDER

WHEN YOU'RE SCARED, really, really scared stiff, when you think, "This, this is it," then your perceptions become doubly keen. The brain switches to red alert—only the here and now count. There's no room for peripheral things. I know that I've reached this state when I cannot even recall my zip code when questioned by the police.

I'm sitting in the interview room of the Iranian police. The furnishings consist of a large desk with a Samsung computer, a lower glass table in the middle of the room, and seven chairs with the plastic wrap still covering the brown leather upholstery. A small door leads to the entrance area and another door to a corridor with further offices. The light green wall is adorned with the national emblem: four crescent moons and a sword. Next to it hang the obligatory portraits of the dictators. Ayatollah Ruhollah Khomeini looks on, sinister as ever. Supreme Leader, Grand Ayatollah Khamenei, however, has a broad grin—I have never seen him look like this. Maybe it's because he is in his element in places like this.

"Two years ago two spies were jailed here," says Yasmin,*
¹my companion. "They're still in jail, in Tehran."

"What did they do?"

"I don't know." But in Iran it's child's play to be considered a
spy. A couple souvenir photos of the airport or a government
building are enough. Or the fact that you travel a bit too close
to the border with Iraq. We are in Nowsud, in Iranian Kurdistan,
and it's only six miles from here to the neighboring country.

"We received a tip-off that there were foreigners here," says
one of the two officials. He is wearing baggy trousers and a
khaki shirt. "Actually, today is our day off," he adds as an explanation for the lack of uniform. Tough face and bulging biceps.
He seems to have spent a lot of time at the gym. His colleague,
dressed in pink, appears mellower, more sympathetic. He has
the beginnings of a paunch under his broad waistband, and
he conveys the impression that the whole procedure is somewhat embarrassing. "Bad Cop" and "Good Cop"—the roles are
clearly defined.

My zip code?

Panic induces me to give the wrong code.

Good Cop asks whether we want some tea. A little while
later a young man in a military uniform brings in a tray. On
drinking I notice that my hand is shaking. Damn. It really
would be better not to show any signs of nervousness.

"Have another look to see if you can find your passport,"
suggests Yasmin. Previously, I had only shown a copy, claiming that the original was at the hotel. In fact, I haven't spent a
single night in a hotel for weeks.

---

* The majority of names have been changed, and last names have
  been omitted to protect the people described.

I rummage around for an appropriate amount of time in the various backpack pockets before producing the required document with feigned surprise. An official in a suit appears from behind me and takes the passport to an adjoining room.

"He'll make some copies and call the immigration authorities to check that everything is okay," explains Yasmin.

On with the interrogation. Cell phone number? Marital status? Father's name?

"Khaki Man" holds on to the printouts and photocopies. Yasmin translates the questions and answers.

"Profession?"

"He's a student," she lies, without consulting me. On my visa application I wrote "website editor," which is nearer the truth.

"Age?"

"Thirty-four."

"What are you studying?" translates Yasmin.

"English and American literature," I answer. That was eight years ago. I chose not to mention the subsequent studies in journalism. Foreign reporters are not too popular among Iranian officials.

"What are you doing here?"

"What is your relationship?"

"He's a friend of my family. He's spending his vacation here," replies Yasmin.

A soldier gathers our luggage from the trunk of the cab and leans them against the glass table in the middle of the room.

"Unpack everything," demands Khaki Man.

On the wall the grin on Supreme Leader Khamenei's face seems to widen. Good teeth for his age—he's over seventy.

3

While extracting the first bags of clothing and a damp towel that smells like a wet dog, my mind goes through everything I have with me.

"Guidebook and Iran books?" Nothing critical in my luggage; the only forbidden book, *Persepolis: The Story of a Childhood*, by Marjane Satrapi,[1] I left in Tehran. Luckily, I don't have any Western news magazines or glossy mags of women without veils.

"Drugs, alcohol, pork?"

"No."

"Notebook?" Very suspicious. I've already filled 2.5 Moleskin notebooks. Conspicuously, on the first page of each booklet I've written: *Iran 1, Iran 2*, and *Iran 3*.

"Press card?" In my wallet. What a bonehead! I should have left it at home.

"Camera?" That could be tricky. Military installations, a nuclear power station, young women without veils, parties with alcohol—everything's there. I could even put a few of my friends at risk. At least a number of particularly sensitive photos are on a smart card that isn't in the camera but hidden in the camera case.

The first article of interest is my toiletry bag, with my first aid kit for travels. The official with baggy pants minutely inspects each pack of pills: Imodium, GeloMyrtol, Aspirin, acetaminophen, Iberogast, Umckaloabo. I'm evidently not a drug smuggler. Then my netbook: turn it on. No suspicious files on my desktop; they are all concealed under innocuous-sounding names. I'm allowed to shut it down. Interest turns to my e-book reader. Handling it clumsily, Khaki Man drops it on the floor, apologizes, and browses through my DuMont Iran art and travel guide. Very touristy, very harmless, very good.

He finds a notepad, this time an Iranian one that a host gave me: *In the name of God, presented to Mr. Stephan during his travel to Lorestan Province, 3.2.1393.* The policeman leafs through all the pages. Apart from the dedication at the front, only blank sheets. I have never received a better present. Luckily, he doesn't find the other notebooks crammed between admission tickets and invoices.

Finished. Pack everything together. I have to restrain myself from taking a deep breath. It wouldn't be such a good idea anyway, as the interview room smells like a particularly nasty damp cloth. I tighten up my backpack straps, sit down on the plastic-covered chair, and reach for my glass of tea. My hand is no longer shaking.

"And now show me your camera," says Khaki Man. And on the wall behind him the Ayatollah Khamenei laughs into his huge beard. He laughs and laughs and laughs.

WELCOME TO IRAN!

"**B**EWARE OF TERRORISTS and kidnappers!" says a friend.

"It's like Saudi Arabia, isn't it? Don't even think about looking any women in the eyes," says a travel journalist.

"Are you going to grow a beard? Bring me back a carpet," says a girlfriend.

"Are you crazy? I just don't understand what you want there," says a colleague from Iran.

Four weeks previously. As soon as the wheels of the TK898 flight from Istanbul touch the runway, a different time scale applies. The Iranian calendar—plus 2.5 hours, minus 621 years. Welcome to Imam Khomeini International Airport: it is 7 *Farvardin* 1393; Happy *Nowruz*; Happy New Year. A rotund man sitting in 14B tips the last drops of his Efes beer down his throat. The teenaged girl in 17F pulls on socks to cover her ankles. Black, blond, brown, red, gray, dyed, styled, groomed, ruffled, short, and long hair all disappear under black, brown, and red scarves. You can tell the foreigners from the Iranians by the way that the unaccustomed piece of cloth slips to the neck on opening the overhead compartments and has to be readjusted. *Respected Ladies: Observe the Islamic dress code* is written on a poster at the terminal—without "please" or "thank you."

Above an illuminated ad for Sony cell phones at the baggage carousel, I am greeted by the first posters of the two bearded ones, ten times larger than life. Ayatollah Ruhollah Khomeini looks wily and somber; even in the photo his eyes seem to penetrate everything. With heightened intellect and infinite frostiness, the leader of the revolution looks down on the world. By contrast, the incumbent Supreme Leader Khamenei, with his large glasses and expressionless eyes, seems almost gawky and harmless, which is remarkable as Ayatollah Khamenei is one of the most powerful and brutal state leaders of recent times.

But then again, maybe this impression is just a question of degree: measured against the gray eminence Ayatollah Khomeini, even Saddam Hussein and Muammar Gaddafi look like nervous *Quran* students revising for exams. The eyes of both ayatollahs seem to say: "From now on we are watching you—wherever you go." The portraits hang in every shop and every restaurant, in residential and government buildings, in mosques, hotels, and bus terminals. In Iran, to avoid the pictures of Ayatollah Khomeini and Ayatollah Khamenei, you have to be in your own apartment or blind.

7 *Farvardin* 1393. As far as the legal situation is concerned, I also have to rethink by a couple hundred years. In Iran *sharia* prevails. In Iran, women, in legal terms, are worth half as much as men and can be stoned to death for adultery. In Iran, I'm a criminal because I have more than three pounds of

Lübeck marzipan (containing a tiny amount of alcohol) and a couple pork cabanossi sausages in my backpack. All that's missing are a couple copies of *Playboy* and I could win a cup with the inscription: *Tehran's Dumbest Entry Attempt.* However, without a few violations of the law, what I plan to do would be impossible. So why not start as I mean to continue? The sooner I get used to my new role as crook, swindler, and actor, the better.

7 *Farvardin* 1393. My cell phone refuses to configure years before 1971 (why 1971?). As punishment for disobeying orders, I insert an Iranian SIM card into the rebellious device. To purchase it I had to sign three forms printed in Persian. I ask the assistant what they contain; he doesn't speak English well.

"No problem!" he replies, and on registering my quizzical look, he repeats, "No problem!" but this time in a gentler, almost friendly, tone.

I desperately need a local SIM card, so I sign. Maybe I have just consented to allow the secret service to monitor all my conversations and text messages, but I couldn't care less. They do it anyway. It even says so in the security information of the State Department.

I have more luck exchanging money. An employee at the cash desk of the Melli Bank tells me that he can give me 35,000 rial per euro, but that one floor higher I will receive 40,000 at the currency exchange there. Eventually, I get 41,500—not a bad rate at all. That's a first for me: I had to travel all the way to Iran to be given sound advice by a banker.

8   I will have plenty of contact with money changers, as the local ATMs don't accept European bank cards. That is pretty impractical for long-term travelers; I am traveling for two months with 2,000 euros and US$1,000 in small

denominations strategically concealed in various inaccessible areas of my luggage. Hopefully, I will remember where they are all hidden when I need money.

The airport with six carousels is smaller than you would expect from a city of 10 million like Tehran. Towering columns, plenty of glass, plenty of concrete. No Starbucks, no McDonald's, no Louis Vuitton, just local fast-food joints, banks, and souvenir shops. A massive poster depicting a goldfish in a bowl—the symbol of life—wishes everyone a Happy New Year. There is probably no other country in the world in which a fish in a bowl symbolizes life.

Whole extended families with bunches of flowers wait for the new arrivals. They got up in the middle of the night to be here on time. It's just after 4 AM. Looking at them I feel very blond and relatively tall. Put it this way: the chances of someone asking me for directions are practically zero.

"Welcome to Iran," say two young women wearing chadors. Chador means "tent" in Persian, which says all you need to know about the nature and femininity of this garment. "Where are you from?" they want to know. "Are you married or single?" Giggling, they then drift away in their ghostly black tents.

Their outfit is not particularly representative at the airport. Most women wear simple headscarves. The younger the person, the more fashionable the color. And the more extended the back of the head seems to be because updos are totally hip. With the scarf covering, it almost looks as though many young Iranian girls have skulls like H.R. Giger's aliens. In comparison, most of the men don't wear any form of head covering. The combination of turban and beard being far less common than Iranian clichés would have us believe. I only see two in the whole terminal.

9

When, after encounters with a benevolent banker and flirta-tious chador girls, a cab driver now refrains from cheating me, I have to readjust my prejudice compass after just one hour in Iran.

There is only one route from the international airport into the city. To the left of the highway 200,000 victims of the Iran-Iraq War are buried in the country's largest cemetery. And opposite, to the right of the highway, rests Ayatollah Khomeini himself, the man who sent so many of them to their deaths. Each of the four towers bordering his grand mausoleum is ninety-one meters (three hundred feet) high, one meter for each year he lived. A huge golden cupola reflects the nighttime spotlight. The first magnificent religious building that tour-ists set their eyes on is the shrine of the ayatollah. The signal that every guest receives is: "This is *my* country, *my* rules apply here"—even twenty-five years after his death.

The cab stops, and the driver doesn't want any money. The trip is for free for a friend like me. I firmly refuse to accept, as required by Iran's complicated rules of courtesy, and he says, "Seventy thousand."

"Rial or toman?" I inquire. There are two currency denomi-nations in Iran, with a zero being the difference, which doesn't make things easier for tourists.

"Toman, of course." Okay, everything times ten.

I give him two 100,000 bills and a 500,000 bill. That's three dollars more than the recommended price to pay that is dis-played on a board at the airport. Charming character, but of course he'll try to cheat you. At least you can rely on the cab drivers.

How to pay in Iran

- Listen to the price.
- Marvel at how cheap it is.
- Convert the named price from rial to toman: add a zero.
- Realize that it isn't so cheap, but still cheaper than home.
- Search for the appropriate bill (count on between thirty and sixty seconds initially).
- Pay.

· · · · · · · · ·

THE MOST STUNNING aspect of Tehran are the nearby Elburz Mountains, reaching up to thirteen thousand feet to the north of the city. The peaks are invisible most weeks of the year because a cloud of smog envelops the city. The daily traffic chaos is legendary; there are almost 4 million cars for the 10 million inhabitants. Most of the almost 4 million exhausts can merely hoarsely laugh at terms like "catalytic converter" or "green fuel." The head of the Traffic Police once calculated that air pollution levels are equivalent to those of 48 million cars with modern exhaust systems. Tehran's motorized pollutants create more carbon monoxide than all automobiles on the streets of Germany. Every year thousands of people die as a result of the smog. It is thought to be healthier to smoke forty cigarettes a day than to spend a few hours wandering around Iran's capital on a smoggy day.

Early in the morning of the New Year celebrations, the gray giant of Tehran is still sleeping. Hardly any traffic, okay views. Behind the Milad Tower, the mountains can be seen as soon as the first light hits them, and there's plenty of snow up there.

In such a slumbering city, whose stores are still shuttered and whose inhabitants are still at home, the first things that catch your eye are the signs. Billboards, signposts, logos. The Persian lettering, with its decorative lines and squiggles, is still unfamiliar. The figure with the highest recognition factor is the "5" as it looks like an upside-down heart.

A barbershop seems to be only able to do eight different styles, at least according to the paintings above the entrance. The ad for a supermarket is less realistic; it depicts a customer and a shopping cart with a single giant apple in it, as big as a medicine ball.

A few feet farther on there is an auto trader shop with a Mercedes star on its facade. It sells Peugeot and Hyundai and Saipa, Iran's own auto brand, but no Mercedes.

There seems to be a disproportionate number of banks in Tehran: Sepah Bank, Pasargad Bank, Samen Credit Institution, Saderat Bank, Melli Bank. There's no point searching for international banking concerns, as a couple years ago UBS, Credit Suisse, and HSBC all withdrew from Iran.

It's still too early to text my host for tonight, so I get out of the cab near the old American Embassy and take a stroll. On both sides of the street there are rows of apartment blocks that look like oversized shoe boxes. Tehran is hiding. From the sidewalk, walls and iron grilles hide the forecourts, windows are made of frosted or reflecting glass, and the curtains are closed to protect against prying eyes.

I walk for ten minutes, not finding a single window to enable me to glimpse the slightest detail of a living room or kitchen. Iran's apartments are the refuges of people with something to hide, strongholds against the outside world. For only when walls surround you can you be free—one of the many paradoxes in the ayatollah's realm.

My trip is a search for the great and small liberties of the Iranians. I'm looking to draw out the mysteries of the country and discover what happens behind the blank windows and closed doors. My ticket to accomplish this I find on online portals like Couchsurfing, Hospitality Club, or BeWelcome, where people offer accommodation to travelers. In Iran there are already more than 160,000 members on Couchsurfing, and the trend is growing rapidly. And all this despite the threat of difficulties with the police for housing foreigners.

The travel guidelines issued by the State Department state: "Iranians are encouraged to have no contact with foreigners 'over and above normal requirements.'" In isolated cases Germans who had organized their accommodation through social networks on the Internet were investigated by the Iranian authorities and promptly deported. "Furthermore: visitors staying overnight with Iranian individuals or families whose addresses have not been registered on the visa application form or at the point of entry must reckon with confiscation of passport and legal procedures."

Before my departure I contacted roughly fifty couchsurfers and a few others I had met during my first trip to Iran a year ago. Most of them replied promptly and gave me their

13

cell phone numbers so that I could contact them en route. I didn't mention any of them on my visa application because so much private contact would have aroused suspicion. One of my acquaintances was refused a visa because he gave the Tehran address of his Iranian friend as his contact address. A few years before, he had had no problems traveling there when he had only entered hotel addresses in tourist locations on his application form.

Two months in a rogue nation, a summer jaunt to the "axis of evil," a vacation in a dictatorship. I don't plan to cross the country from east to west or north to south or to allow myself to be governed by the guidebook tips and must-see tourist attractions. Where I go depends on people. I have planned a rough route, but I am prepared to ditch it at any time if the Iranians have better suggestions. And if they have worse ideas, I will still join in. When in Qom, do as the Qomans do. Or something like that.

My travel destination is assimilation. Within the next few weeks I want to morph from a blond Westerner to an Iranian— well, at least to a certain extent. The to-do list is: 1. Unveil mysteries. 2. Become an Iranian. 3. Get out alive.

To: Yasmin Tehran
Hey Yasmin, how are you, my dear? This is my iranian number. When can I come to your place?

To: Masoud Kish
Hey Masoud, this is Stephan from cs, how are you? I will arrive on Kish in a few days, could you host me for 1 or 2 nights? Would be great!:)

DOWN WITH THE U.S.

BREAKFAST TIME. I go to the first convenient café, where a few laborers from a construction site are sitting. There is only one meal on the menu, a fatty soup with calf's brain. Tender meat is usually something delicate, but this is just a bit too tender for my tastes. Lesson of the day: 8:30 isn't a good time for food experiments. But everyone else seems to like it. Evidence that the assimilation that I am seeking is as distant as Isfahan is from Illinois. This also applies to the language. Apart from "hello," "bye," "tea," and "thanks," I can say *almani*, meaning "German," and *Man farsi balad nistam*—"I don't speak Persian." The last sentence I apparently pronounce so well that the brain soup restaurant owner doesn't believe me and proceeds to fire off a wide-ranging barrage of small talk. The conversation remains one-sided and eventually he accepts that I've understood nothing.

People staying in hotels can simply check in at any time. For someone staying in a private apartment the situation is more complicated. You have to adjust to when your host is

at home; you have to synchronize with the daily patterns. As I booked my flight on very short notice, I couldn't fix a time to meet Yasmin. *Contact me when you have landed,* she posted on Facebook. Until I receive a reply to my text message, I'm a homeless person with heavy luggage.

The neighborhood is well known for its propaganda art. DOWN WITH USA is written in screaming capitals on a wall near the former American Embassy. A couple feet away there is a mural of the Statue of Liberty with the glittering silver spiky crown perched on a skull. Next to it is a picture of the Capitol Building, with Israel's flag flying above the cupola. I knew about this graffiti from reports about Iran; they are popular subjects for typifying Tehran. Most of these reports are about religious fanatics, plans to build an atomic bomb, and hate-filled tirades against America or Israel. In the rankings of countries with the worst image, Iran has been striving for the World Cup title for years.

"Welcome to Iran," I hear a voice next to me say. The stranger in the suit doesn't seem to fit the murals—he really means it.

A quick call to Yasmin; she doesn't answer. I walk to the House of the Artists, just a few blocks away. According to the guidebook it is a good place to get in contact with local artists, and those are not the ones who paint the walls with anti-American slogans. Unfortunately, the museum is closed for the New Year celebrations, as is the adjoining café. I find a bench in the park, lean my backpack against it, and doze off.

From: Yasmin Tehran
Hi, i told you no problem with time, always welcome

She answers my text message in the afternoon, and I take a cab to the southern Eskandari Street. We shake hands. She is wearing a black top with a glittery silver Eiffel Tower motif and a baseball cap on top of her veil.

"How are you? Anything new?" she asks. I got to know Yasmin during my first Iran trip a year ago.

We turn into a small side street, go through a squeaking iron door into the forecourt, where two white Saipas are parked, then up the concrete staircase to the first story. I take my shoes off, hug Yasmin's mother, hand over the box of marzipan, and put the luggage into my room. I know where everything is from my last visit.

Her mother is wearing a string top and no veil. As soon as the door is closed, Yasmin, despite having a male visitor, takes off her veil, revealing short dyed blond hair.

According to the official government figures, 99 per cent of Iranians are Muslims, but Yasmin's family is not religious. At home she doesn't have to behave as if there is a thick curtain at the living room window, excluding both light and curious gazes. I'm offered hot tea, nuts, and Chichak chocolate bars, with a wrapper closely resembling a Snickers. I feel at home. The Iranians are masters at making visitors feel as comfortable as possible.

17

The TV is broadcasting a speech by the Iranian leader Ayatollah Khamenei. The most powerful figure in the country is waving around his cue card, hollering into two microphones about how the Iranians shouldn't kowtow to the Americans, the Yanks are stealing oil, something has to be done about it. Instead of using his cue card, he could just as well have read out the messages on the walls of the former U.S. Embassy. Without Ayatollah Khomeini next to him, he actually seems to be ever so slightly charismatic. But only ever so slightly.

"There's always a speech like this on Fridays," says Yasmin.

"Today's Thursday."

"It's a repeat, so that we all remember that tomorrow we will get the same speech with different words." And then to her mother: "Hey, come on, switch channels."

Her mother obeys. First she switches to a program about the correct way to arrange roses and then to a music channel playing "G.U.Y" by Lady Gaga. The singer's dress is white, but so scant that "color of innocence" is not what comes to mind. I ask Yasmin why Iranians hate the U.S.

"Not the Iranians—the government," she replies. "Many young people dream of emigrating to America because it's a free country. However, some people believe that the CIA secretly determines Iran's future, as it has already done repeatedly in the past. During the presidential elections, time and again, rumors abound about America manipulating the results."

"Then they did a pretty good job this time," I quip.

During my last trip Mahmoud Ahmadinejad, whom a German newspaper dubbed the "Madman of Tehran," was president. Now the moderate Hassan Rouhani has been in office for several months. In the background, Ayatollah Khamenei continues to pull the strings—a point that is often forgotten because he is rarely present on the international stage.

"Why do all Europeans think Rouhani is so great?" asks Yasmin.

"Because he's a good speaker and seems pretty reasonable. At least compared to his crazy predecessor, who was quite capable of shooting himself in the foot at every UN General Assembly. You're not convinced by him?"

"Nothing much has changed in the last year. The moral police are still active, prices rise, and the relationship to America hasn't improved."

"But there have been diplomatic breakthroughs—the sanctions have been relaxed, and for the first time in thirty-five years the Iranian and American leaders have been in telephone contact."

"There's been much talk and little action. Rouhani comes from the same clerical stock as Khomeini and Khamenei. He just pretends to be more modern and liberal. He is a master of fine words, but apart from that, he's achieved precious little," she answers.

Yasmin is thirty-one, a touch chubby, paints ladybugs on her nails, and can alternate between talking seriously and exploding into laughter within a split second. She longs for the trade restrictions to be lifted. Since Iran was barred from the SWIFT financial network in March 2012, the country has been practically cut off from international money transactions. And there have been less foreign imports, including essential medications, since then.

"I have a bone disease and am dependent on medication that isn't available here. I hope that next year I can get a grant to study for my doctoral thesis in Germany. I just want to get out of this country."

She has completed her studies as a software engineer and is now working on her master's thesis in tourism management.

19

Her main topic is the battlefields of the Iran-Iraq War and the stream of visitors there. Every year, millions of Iranians travel to the memorials. Her father could probably help her with the subject, as he was a naval officer. Just now he is on a trip to southwest Iran with a few other war veterans, visiting places where they fought.

I have to get on the Internet to write to a couple prospective hosts and to book a flight to Kish Island. The computer is in the room that is mine for the next couple days—two beds with floral bedspreads, a wooden closet, a chest of drawers crammed to the top with all sorts of odds and ends, no window. Normally, this is Yasmin's room, but she has moved into her mother's room.

Yasmin closes the Facebook tab on her browser. Officially, the website is banned in Iran. Still, I have never met an Iranian under thirty-five who isn't on Facebook; they use proxy servers to access it. Yasmin helps me with the flight arrangements; domestic flights are not easy to book.

"Do you want to pay less and fly with a Fokker or pay more for a Boeing?" she asks.

"A Fokker is okay," I answer.

As you read Persian from right to left, it seems to me that the times on the flight website are the wrong way around. The Fokker flight on Sunday, for instance, appears to depart at 15:10 and arrive at 13:15. She reserves a ticket for me that I can collect the day after tomorrow at the travel center.

"Do you want to visit a couple battlefields during your stay? We could go there together. In three weeks," suggests Yasmin. The first day, the first change in plans. I accept the proposal immediately.

Her mother rolls out a plastic sheet, also with a floral design, on the living room carpet and places on it bowls with small meatballs and potatoes together with pita bread and *dugh*, a sour milk drink similar to Turkish *ayran*.

"Do you remember this? At last year's New Year celebration you spilled it all over your T-shirt," says Yasmin grinning.

How to behave while eating

- Sit cross-legged on the floor.
- Wait for the starting orders: "*Bokhor, bokhor!*"
- Tear off a rectangular piece of the pita bread.
- Fill it with the main course and roll it up.
- Bite into it.
- Try to surreptitiously pick up bits of food that have landed on the carpet (they *never* land on the plastic sheet).

· · · · · · · · · ·

THE TV IS on nonstop, and now there is a report about a bus of battleground pilgrims driving over a mine and exploding in the area that Yasmin's father is now visiting. She is worried about him because he hasn't been in touch since this morning and isn't taking calls.

"How can a bus drive over a twenty-five-year-old mine? Haven't the roads been cleared of the things for years?" I inquire.

"The bus hit a car and veered off the road, triggering a land mine from the war. Incredibly unlucky."

Yasmin's mother is understandably not enthusiastic about our plan. She tries for the umpteenth time to reach her husband without success. "It's pretty out of the way. Reception is sure to be bad," she says.

Yasmin changes the topic.

"Do you want to join me on Sunday for a very special meeting? Something absolutely forbidden?"

"Sure, what's it all about?"

"A special kind of relationship."

"How special?"

"*Very* special."

"A more precise description would be helpful."

"Have you heard about BDSM? Bondage games? Sadomasochism? It's hard to imagine anything more forbidden in Iran. We meet in a park. Slaves, masters, and a dominatrix."

"*Aha.*"

"I knew that you wouldn't say no!"

LONG LIVE THE SHAH

BUT FIRST OF all some history lessons are on the program. The next day we visit the National Museum of Iran, which is considered by those in the know to be the *mother of all museums*, at least that is what is written on a poster on the outer wall. The exhibits are in fact sensational. Who knew that the Persians turned out the first cartoon in the world, with emphasis on *turned*? It is on a round earthen goblet depicting an ibex jumping toward a tree and eating its leaves. The picture consists of five individual images, and if you turn the goblet quickly enough it gives the impression of animation, somewhat similar to a flip-book.

At the Academy Awards in 2300 BC *Ibex Eats Leaves* would have racked up the Oscars in all categories: screenplay, director, visual effects, score (the sound of clay rubbing on a sandy surface), and best supporting role (the tree). Unfortunately, there were no Oscars then. Cultural events in Germany at that time? A couple long-haired cave dwellers spinning old hunter yarns at the fireside. Cultural events in America at that time? Well, you get the picture. A feast for cineasts is also the sculptured throne scene from the Achaemenid era depicting King Darius and his son Xerxes. Both have sensational beards and are holding lotus blossoms. Light-headed from the fumes of two incense burners, they receive representatives from a distant province. When the stone relief was chiseled out at around 500 BC, Persia was the first superpower in history, with an empire ranging from India to the Danube. Today's countries of Turkey, Syria, Egypt, Libya, Pakistan, and Afghanistan all belonged to Darius's gigantic empire. A network of roads was created stretching thousands of miles, with countless caravanserai for travelers. And the first postal system in history.

However, in the subsequent centuries, you had to be careful when deciding on domestic or international rates. Time and again the borders shifted due to various wars, various battles, and various conquerors. First, there was Alexander the Great. Then the Parthians, and the Sasanians, followed by the Arabs, Genghis Khan, Tamerlane, the Safawids. Good shahs and bad shahs, and finally, in the twentieth century, the shahs of the Pahlavi dynasty, eventually leading to the revolution with ayatollahs Khomeini and Khamenei. Already in 1979, when the

24

mullahs came to power, Persia, on the way from global empire to religious dictatorship, had suffered more at the hands of unscrupulous tyrants than most other nations.

The next history lesson of the day wouldn't have happened if I had been traveling alone. I simply would have missed the finer details on the Bagh-e Melli Gate. The magnificent entrance to a former military parade ground was built during the reign of Reza Shah Pahlavi in 1922, with huge doors with floral designs made from cast iron. Hand-painted ornate tiles depict idyllic landscapes and deadly weapons. Meadows, forests, lakes, and country houses with red roofs provide the background for depictions of Vickers machine guns between Iranian flags.

"Do you notice anything?" asks Yasmin.

"It would look quite nice without the weapons."

"I don't mean that; look at the flags."

"The crescent moon in the middle of the white stripe is missing. And there are truncated golden animal legs on the lower red stripe."

"Exactly! The lion was painted over—it was the national emblem of Iran during the time of the two Pahlavi shahs."

25

"And there was no money left for red paint, which is why the legs remain?"

"Probably. Do you see the metal crest above the door?"

"Looks as if half of it was sawed off."

"There was also a lion there, and below it the inscription *Long Live the Shah*. Ayatollah Khomeini had a metal plate superimposed, so that all that remains is *Long Live*.

"Is censorship always so easy to spot?"

"Would that it were. But luckily, not everyone is as blind as you," she says.

At the last stop in today's history triathlon, the Golestan Palace and its parks, the lions have survived. There are so many of them that they would have needed more than just a bit of white paint. Most of the lions seem to be busy pouncing on ibexes or dragons. Such motifs symbolize the victory of Persia against her adversaries and were much loved by the shahs who lived here from the eighteenth to the twentieth century.

Yasmin then tells me of the most foolish shah of all—Naser al-Din Shah Qajar, in the second half of the nineteenth century. He believed, for example, that red was his color, and nobody else was allowed to wear anything red. "On top of that, he was a passionate collector who was always swapping whole Persian cities for works of art." Fourteen cabinets of finest porcelain from Russia, England, and Germany are displayed in a room of the palace. "Each cabinet was a city," explains Yasmin. She always has a story on hand that you can't find in history books. "Once he was so drunk that he even wanted to swap Tehran, until, at the very last moment, one of his advisers pointed out that it was the capital of the country."

The interior of the palace is not only proof of his mania for collecting but also of his narcissism, and there are a couple

26

hundred tiles showing the shah hunting. His tombstone, not far away, is an effigy of the shah with a sensational mustache. A protective screen has been placed above it, which is covered with pigeon droppings. Every day pigeons drop their loads on the shah, and the eyes of the effigy follow the flight paths of every plane. There must be better ways to spend eternity.

The last shah of Persia, Mohammad Reza Shah Pahlavi, was crowned at Golestan Palace and guided the affairs of state from 1941 until the revolution in 1979. He was more conciliatory toward the Muslim clergy than his father, lifting, for example, the ban on chadors. But his extravagant lifestyle, his controversial politics, and his cozy relationship to the West brought him many enemies. At some stage the situation became untenable, and the people took to the streets, paving the way for the seizure of power by the *mullahs*. The shah was forced into exile, and Ayatollah Khomeini returned from exile and received a hero's welcome.

Those who pause after the sensory overload of halls of mirrors, treasure chambers, and all the accentuation on marble unavoidably come to the conclusion that being a shah couldn't have been too bad a way to spend your time. I ask Yasmin to rate my chances of this career path. This induces a high-pitched fit of laughter, and then she points to an inner courtyard, where a photographer takes photos in authentic regal regalia. Touristy folklore, but it's worth the five dollars for two pictures.

I don a green silk frock coat, a blue cloak with embroidered flowers, a round, flat cap with a feather. An assistant quickly glues on my mustache. Several other visitors stop by and greet me with "Welcome to Iran!" Gradually, more and more onlookers gather to follow my photo session. Should I use the window of opportunity to gain a few potential subjects?

27

I nod gracefully toward them, slowly raising my silk-covered arm in a greeting and smiling with dignity. From the tension of my skin the mustache becomes dislodged and with it every imagined aura of majesty. The onlookers, however, are royally amused. My lesson for today: shahs don't smile.

COUCHSURFING FOR
BEGINNERS

THE NEXT DAY I take the number one line north. A well-groomed man in a shirt and suit pants with a hairstyle like American football quarterback Tom Brady sits next to me. First he speaks to me in Persian and then English. He only needs five minutes to tell me what's wrong with his country.

I learn that he is fifty, works as an electrician for a company making machines, and earns US$200 a month. "You can't live on that; it's just about enough to cover the rent. There's no chance of getting married, either." And then he becomes astonishingly open and intimate. "You know, for us sex is a real problem. Those without money can't marry, and anyhow nothing goes on before marriage. Everything has got much worse since the financial crisis. Hardly anyone can afford to have a couple kids. And at the same time we can't get our asses into gear. I'm not the exception there. I sit on the couch after work and watch TV because there's nothing better to do. Iranians are incredibly friendly, but once you become better acquainted with them you will see the darker sides. Envy, for example, when someone else has more. And the lack of a fighting spirit: people try to come to terms with their lot, to make the best of their circumstances, but not to fight for or against something. Have a nice day. Welcome to Iran!"

I get out at Mofatteh and look for Raam Café at the corner of Mehrdad Street and Aslipur Street. I'm a little bit late, and some twenty young people are sitting in a circle of chairs. The round of introductions has already started.

"My name is Mehedi. I'm twenty-eight and have been a member for three or four days and work as a tourist guide. I don't like hotels, as they don't have anything human about them, anything individual. I like traveling simply, without luggage."

"I'm Atafeh, twenty-four years old, and a member for a couple months. I'd like to meet Iranians who can show me their cities. I love surprises."

"Neda, twenty-nine. I've been registered for four weeks and have used couchsurfing in Germany. You can make many friends by traveling like this."

"Stephan from Germany. I've been couchsurfing for more than ten years and have had roughly 80 guests and 120 hosts. I can't imagine traveling without couchsurfing."

The café sports designer wooden shelves full of books. A *Chinatown* movie poster hangs on the wall; Nescafé is served, and so are nonalcoholic mojitos. The atmosphere is of a Bible class. Or a self-help group. Or a sect. Two dozen people between twenty and forty have come to experience how couchsurfing works. Their guru is called Pedram, a charismatic bald guy with a MacBook and an Adidas T-shirt, who drinks water from a bike bottle when there is a lull in conversation, which is seldom. On an almost-daily basis he organizes some meeting or other. Free tours of the city, photography walks, visits to museums. And every fortnight he organizes a meeting for beginners, today for the tenth time.

"I will talk about the basics, the rules, about surfing and hosting, and about security," he announces. Pedram doesn't have to worry about running out of enthusiasts. "A year ago couchsurfing had a few thousand members, and now we have more than 100,000."

A red-haired girl, her scarf way above her forehead, asks: "If we visit strangers that we only know from the Internet, how can we trust them?"

"A very important question. Trust is of utmost importance," Pedram replies. "One general rule is to go through the profile very carefully before you arrange to meet. Trust your gut feelings, your instincts—sometimes you will feel that something isn't quite right. And there are reviews. If you are hosting or surfing, leave a short comment."

The red-haired girl asks me about my worst experience. I tell her about a visitor from Frankfurt who wanted to talk the whole night about the intricacies of high-end stereo systems, although I had to get up the next morning at eight and had an important exam at the university, and in addition to that he behaved as if he were in a hotel with twenty-four-hour butler service.

"That was your worst experience?" she asks incredulously.

"Yes, and the second worst was the guest who stole my toilet paper."

So, all within the bounds of reason.

From: Masoud Kish

Hello Stephan, I have the in-laws here, but might kick them out to host you. Just call me when you arrive ok?

TORTURE

LUSH GREEN TREETOPS sway in the wind, a fountain softly splutters, traffic whirs from the main road. A young couple, holding hands, stroll along the freshly tarred path. Tehran's couples hold hands in public in parks when they feel safe from critical eyes. Teenagers, with hoodies and Justin Bieber hairstyles, display their skateboarding skills on the high curbs. They tumble and pick themselves up without seeming to feel pain, all the while listening to music on their headphones—boom boxes are forbidden. Two older men are torturing themselves on open-air exercise equipment made of colorful metal.

It is a mild spring Sunday in Goftegoo Park, the name meaning something like "chatter," and that's just what we are doing. Farshad explains that religious names for children have become less popular in recent years. "People question belief more nowadays; not everyone is called Mohamad or Hussein." He is pleased with his name, which means "happy."

Amir asks me how I'm enjoying Iran. I praise the friendliness of the people and the museums and palaces. Yasmin explains to all how funny I looked in the shah costume. Only Kaveh ambles silently beside us; he speaks little English and is in a bad mood because someone stole his wallet in the subway.

Five of us saunter to a café in the middle of the park. From the terrace we have a magnificent view of the Elburz mountain range, whose white peaks tower above the sea of houses and the top of the Milad Tower, one of the tallest TV towers in the world. Below the railings there is an artificial lake with concrete banks, where small children check out the fat ducks and make quacking noises. We move three plastic tables, numbered 33, 34, and 35, together, as we are expecting more guests. Then we sit down and order water and tea.

We made the introductions at the entrance to the park. Now follows the second round: one after the other, Yasmin points to Farshad, Amir, Kaveh, and herself. "Slave, Master, Master, Mistress," she says. Then, grinning, she points toward me and adds: "Undecided."

Yasmin organized the meeting via an Internet forum. If the police realized what we were speaking about, we would be arrested. The plan for the next hour? "We start off with the theory and then test it out on you," suggests the slave Farshad. "We could strap you to the table and then show you something about Iranian hospitality." Two Masters and a Mistress buckle with laughter. I join in rather sheepishly.

I prefer Yasmin's version of the day's schedule: "We will discuss our relationships, techniques, and… er… just about everything else," she says. The group meets every month at a different venue, which Yasmin announces only a few hours beforehand. "Meeting at home wouldn't be possible with so many people; it would be too conspicuous."

Farshad is thirty-two, with neatly combed hair kept in place with hair gel and gentle brown eyes, and is wearing a light blue shirt. "You know, we see allusions everywhere. Look, your water is called *oxub*. That sounds like a shortened form of 'submission.' You could also make a fine strap-on dildo from the bottle, a bit on the large size, but it'd only hurt at the beginning and pretty soon you'd be in a trance."

Farshad asks me what I know about BDSM. I say it's about dominance, role-playing, and pain, and I know the enthusiasm of the Iranian clergy toward it is not overwhelming. "It's crazy, really, when you consider that Imam Husayn fought for freedom, but there's no freedom for us," says Amir, a man in peak condition, with round glasses and a bald head. Iran's Shiites venerate Husayn, grandson of the Prophet Muhammad, who died for his beliefs at the legendary Battle of Karbala. Every year during *Muharram* (the first month of the Islamic calendar), Shiites mourn his death, and some devotees practice the tradition of self-flagellation.

"Hasn't that also got something sadomasochistic about it?" I ask.

"Sometimes. Believers want to repent, to free themselves from their sins via pain," explains Farshad. In the meantime, self-flagellation is officially forbidden, but this does not in any way deter people from practicing it. Every year the ritual is repeated.

"For me it's not about repentance, but rather about passing on responsibility to someone else," says Farshad, who is employed by a law firm. "The most important thing is trust. You can compare it to a bird in a cage; it is completely dependent on the owner, totally at his mercy. This external domination can be very relaxing; afterward you feel reborn."

35

Give me a dictator who can convince me that he means well, and I will follow him.

Amir adds: "It's all about switching off logical thought, simply to feel that even something irrational can be pleasant. Many people repress this. But the success of *Fifty Shades of Grey*[1] shows how many secretly feel it."

"Can you buy the book here?" I ask.

"Of course not. Nobody here would be allowed to read it."

Now and then the conversation drifts into Persian, and then I only understand a few English words like "sadist," "domination," or "submission." There does not appear to be adequate Persian words for such terms. Farshad notices that I'm struggling to follow the conversation. "We're just discussing what we are going to do with you," he explains with the heartiest laugh imaginable.

Two newcomers shake hands with the group. Shahin, a shy writer. "My first slave a few years ago," Yasmin whispers to me. And Babak, a journalist for a news agency. "He's a switch," she explains. "Sometimes Master, sometimes Slave." The young man apologizes for being late; he was detained by the police— not because of the meeting, just a spot check. His car was combed for drugs and alcohol: the trunk, seats, glove box, foot mats, the works.

Directly in front of the entrance to the park are the law enforcers, with an army tent and machine guns. Now and then a the park is patrolled by a policeman, which we can observe from our terrace. But being searched doesn't seem to have perturbed a man like Babak, not even on the way to a forbidden SM meeting. Soon after, the subject changes to Iran's places of interest.

"You want to visit the country? Then you must go to Kermanshah, to the mountains of Farhad and Shirin," suggests Babak. He doesn't speak English, so Yasmin has to translate.

"Who are Farhad and Shirin?" I want to know, and he begins to explain.

"In the mountains of Kurdistan there lived a simple stonemason named Farhad, who fell in love with Princess Shirin. One day she heard him play his flute in the open air, and she fell for him, although they weren't from the same class. Khosrow II, the then king of the Persian Empire, also revered the princess. When he heard rumors of her infatuation with a commoner, he hatched a plan to separate the lovers. He ordained that Farhad had to perform an impossible task to prove himself worthy of Shirin's hand. 'Cut a forty-mile tunnel through the mountain between two valleys in Kurdistan, and then you can have her for your wife,' he said. Farhad shouldered his tools and set about his task.

"Every day from dawn to dusk he hammered away at the rock face with his pickax and shovel, month after month, year after year. Sometimes when he slept, Shirin would secretly visit him to view the progress. He slept on the naked mountainside, using his shovel as a pillow. Shirin's heart warmed as she saw that every fifteen feet he had sculpted a statue of her in the rock, so great was his love. So hard did he work that after many, many years it looked as if he might finish his task. Khosrow, of course, wanted to prevent this, so he ordered a gathering of his viziers to concoct a plan. The advisers suggested sending an old lady to Farhad to tell him that Shirin had died. Then he would be sure to abandon his work.

"So the next morning an old lady approached the doughty stonemason. She wailed and wept, and Farhad asked her the

37

reason for her suffering. 'I'm mourning a death—and for you,' she answered.

"'Why is that, then?' he asked, astonished.

"'Brave man, you have worked so solidly, but it was all in vain. The object of your affections is dead.'

"Farshad's heart was heavy with despair. He threw his shovel into the air and it landed on his neck, mortally wounding him. His blood flowed into the channel that he had hewn with so much effort. When Shirin heard the news she immediately left for the mountains. She saw her dead lover, grabbed the shovel, and in anguish aimed a blow to her head. To this day the two lovers lie together high up in the mountains of Kurdistan, and to this day on Mount Bisotun you can see where Farhad worked away at the rock face out of love for Shirin."

Farshad sighs audibly and seems moved, although he must have heard the tale many times. "There are many love stories in literature, but that is the only one that is about pure, unconditional love," he says. Only then do I realize the similarity in names.

As a slave he deems it difficult to find a partner in Iran. In a country where women, from a legal point of view, are second-class citizens, dominatrices are apparently particularly sought after.

"There are far too few of us. I get so many requests on the Internet that I could have twenty slaves all at once," says Yasmin. However, she has no need of them because she has been in a steady relationship for nine months. She regularly posts on Facebook sites that are only accessible to members, photos of bondage games in the jungle or sessions in her torture chamber, in a house in northern Iran. In the scene, she has quite a reputation.

"Shall we go inside?" she suggests. "It's getting cold."

"Doesn't bother me; I'm a masochist," jokes Babak.

Nevertheless, we move indoors to the lower level restaurant, where you sit without shoes upon raised platforms and paintings of bazaars hang on the walls. Master Kaveh, nicknamed "Rough," places a cushion behind me and makes room so that I'm comfortable. Over Istak malt beer and *kofta* meatballs we chat about Tehran's traffic problems, Kafka, and homemade erotic accessories carved from wood.

Politics isn't discussed—well, only once, briefly: "Up to now they have left our online group in peace. It would be very different if we were a discussion forum critical of the state," says Farshad. "Unusual sexual practices are bad in Iran, but political activism is ten times worse."

Finally, we take a little stroll through Goftegoo Park. Shirvin and Amir discuss whips and handcuffs. Farshad tells me about the board game Femdomopoly—femdom for female domination, where the throw of dice decides the type of pain or humiliation the player has to withstand. Yasmin and the writer Shahin separate from the group, chatting and walking hand in hand in the park. Only when I look very carefully do I notice that while doing this, she is digging her very sharp fingernails into the palm of his hand. Both walk past the artificial lake in which a few goldfish swim; here the goldfish are free. And at the park entrance you see the police and their machine guns and army tent, as if there were a border crossing here that needed surveillance, instead of a very ordinary park, where people gather to chat, somewhere in Tehran.

How to cross roads in Iran

- Wait at the roadside until the nearside lane is free.
- Notice in astonishment that suddenly important moments in your life are flashing through your mind.
- Beginners: seek out a group of locals and follow their movements in their slipstream.
- Proceed swiftly but without haste; keep you head at a ninety-degree angle to the direction you're headed.
- Avoid abrupt movements.
- When calculating speed and trajectory *never* expect braking maneuvers.
- Especially not at pedestrian crossings. Pedestrian crossings are traps!
- Drivers are quite prepared to swerve to left or right when there is little traffic. It is considered less of an effort to turn the steering wheel slightly than to move your foot from the accelerator to the brake pedal.
- Evaluate feedback: If you are hooted at two or three times, everything's okay. Four or more times means there's room for improvement in tempo and/or body language. If you don't hear any hooting for thirty seconds, you're dead.

FREEDOM

THE FLIGHT FOR the vacation island of Kish takes off from Mehrabad International Airport. A modern terminal with sparkling clean halls, neon lights, and billboards advertising luxury apartments. On small tables there are chargers for all types of cell phones. I have never heard of most of the airlines: Mahan Air, Caspian Airlines, Iran Aseman Airlines. Kish Airlines is on my ticket, filled out by hand by the assistant at the travel agency. On the wall there is a poster of Ayatollah Khomeini, with a particularly sinister look and the inscription *Have a Nice Trip* next to his head. When the ayatollah landed at just this airport thirty-five years ago on an Air France flight, millions of Iranians cheered his return from exile. They had succeeded in booting the hated shah off his Peacock Throne. But many of the revolutionaries became bitterly disappointed in the ensuing years, as the ayatollah proved to be an uncompromising despot who may well have ruled his Islamic Republic without the pomp and excess of his predecessor but with the same brutality.

I wander through the halls and try to wait for the right moment to take an unobserved snapshot of the poster. It is forbidden to take photos at airports, stations, or any government buildings.

A passenger with a chador and neatly plucked eyebrows interprets my movements differently. "Are you lost? Do you need help?" she asks.

"No thanks. I'm just looking around," I reply.

"Welcome to Iran," she continues and introduces herself as Solmaz, thirty-five; she has a master's degree in philosophy and dreams of writing her thesis in Sweden. She is now flying to Mashhad to pray at the shrine to Imam Reza.

"Are you traveling alone? Aren't you a bit lonely?" she asks.

"Not at all. You never feel alone here as tourist."

Fear of the lack of human contact in Iran is like a round-the-world yachtsman being worried about getting a suntan.

"Yes, we're good to foreigners," she says pensively.

"Are you coming back to Tehran?"

"Yes, in six or seven weeks."

"I can show you the city, inshallah."

She compliments me for choosing to visit Kish and recommends a trip in a glass-bottom boat. And the water park. And the dolphinarium. "They have dolphins there that can clean their teeth." We swap phone numbers and then my flight is called.

From the plane window Iran's number one vacation destination looks like a ten-mile-wide ellipse made of white sand and flat as a beach towel. But what the island lacks in natural elevation it makes up for with a whole host of domino-like skyscrapers in the northeast. Kish needs these hotel complexes to cater to the 1.5 million tourists who visit the island annually. What the Dominican Republic is for Americans, Kish is for Persians. They love the island and return here for their vacations time and again. The guidebook states: "There are not many reasons to come here for non-Iranians." So, the perfect place to begin my transformation to an Iranian. My plane lands on the heat-shimmering asphalt of the desert island's airport.

While Tehran's Mehrabad International Airport epitomizes modern Iran, the airport at Kish is more like a teeny disco between two car rental booths. To the droning sounds of techno music, two B-boys, completely coated in silver paint, go through their pirouette routines considerably more supplely than the summer jobbers in SpongeBob and pink elephant costumes a few feet away, clowning about with kids. They must be sweating terribly in their woolen slippers. To remind the new arrivals that they are in Iran and not in Disneyland, a huge map of the surrounding waters is painted on the wall flanked by grim portraits of ayatollahs Khomeini and Khamenei. Below the map, the slogan *Persian Gulf Forever* is a special message to visitors from Arabian countries. The name, which has existed for centuries, is disputed, and the southerly neighbors want to rename it the Arabian Gulf. Those who say,

43

"What's the problem? It's just a name" don't know the national pride of the Iranians. For them it would be a slap in the face if they were to lose their only sea. The Caspian Sea in the north doesn't count, as it's actually a lake. My host, Masoud, wrote in his text message that he would try to accommodate me, and I should contact him on landing. So, I call his number. A friendly, deep telephone voice says, "What's up, bro?" in flawless American slang and goes on to say that he will call me back in a few minutes with instructions about where to go.

Another passenger, after five minutes of small talk, uses my waiting time to invite me to his wedding in northern Iran. Unfortunately, the date clashes with my trip to the battlefields with Yasmin, so with a heavy heart I have to turn down the invitation. And then again. And once more.

How to *taarof*—understanding politeness

Iranians sometimes offer you the most amazing things. Free cab rides, carpets for nothing, gratis goods at the bazaar. Those who don't recognize these as gestures of politeness are about to put their foot in it—and deep.

The rule: always politely decline twice. When the offer comes for the third time you can be sure that it really is meant seriously and can be accepted without loss of face to your partner.

Tricky: even the phrase *taarof nemikonam!*—no *taarof*—can be thought of as *taarof*.

44

· · · · · · · · ·

MASOUD SENT ME a text message, including directions, which I was to show to the cab driver. Unfortunately, my cell phone doesn't recognize Persian letters, so I go to the nearest bright yellow cab and call Masoud, handing the phone to the cab driver. The cab passes stony, derelict land with rows of palm trees and roundabouts with neatly clipped eucalyptus trees and sculpted sea creatures. The cars are larger and more modern than in Tehran, and there are fewer Saipa and Peugeot, but instead more Hyundai, Toyota and a few Mercedes. The streets and sidewalks are as clean as if they were vacuumed last night, a huge contrast to the barrenness all around.

The cab driver stops in the newly built district of Arabar, in the western section of the island. The townhouses made from veined and polished blocks of stone give an appearance of money and coldness reminiscent of Dubai. It really is a new district; half of the street is still a construction site.

"A couple years ago there was nothing here," says Masoud, a suntanned guy in a gray polo shirt, who appeared at the door after my latest phone call. Angular face, bushy eyebrows, tidy blow-dried hairdo. He is a flight dispatcher for Iran Aseman Airways, working as an English teacher on the side.

"Would you like a cup of tea?"

He leads me up to the first floor. Masoud's sister, Mahbube, a hairdresser, is sitting on an orange polka-dot sofa with her two children, Saler and Saba, thirteen and eleven. Masoud's wife is also named Mahbube, so I memorize her as Mahbube 2. She brings in black tea and sand-colored cookies. She is an architect and is now studying art and drawing. Both women and the girl wear head coverings the whole time we are in the apartment. They are doing this solely because of me, the presence of a male guest, as all the rest are family.

"We have a full house today, but somehow we will manage, even with six of us," says Masoud cheerfully.

45

The apartment is about 430 square feet. It consists of only a living room with a separate kitchen, a bedroom, and a bathroom. The walls are bare except for one *Quran* sura inscribed on silver foil.

A forty-two-inch LG TV, made in South Korea, dominates the room. At the moment it is showing an imam who is singing so out of tune that his listeners in the mosque begin to wail. I present my interpretation of what is going on to Masoud.

"Nonsense! It's a very sad story. He is preaching about the death of the martyr Husayn," says Masoud.

He then changes the subject. "Do you like *Flight Simulator?*" He connects a special joystick and two speakers to his laptop.

"Let's fly over Germany. What's a nice short route?"

"Hamburg to Berlin," I suggest.

Shortly afterward we are flying together in an Airbus A330 to Berlin, and I'm getting a crash course in the cockpit. "Ground speed: 250 miles per hour; altitude: 6,000 feet; direction 110," he announces, pointing to the corresponding dials. "Berlin is simple; they have an instrument landing system. But here not all the airports are equipped with it." It is not possible to import modern technology because of the sanctions, and spare parts for airplanes are also a problem. "That's why we have more accidents here than in other countries," he adds. As evidence he loads the Urmia to Tabriz route in northwest Iran. Majestic mountains, severe turbulence. On landing, without the aid of an instrument landing system, he promptly demolishes the front wheel. "You see! That's what sanctions do."

Kish is an island of shopping centers. We spend the early evening in massive shopping malls made of concrete and steel, named Paradise I, Paradise II, or Kish Trade Center. On offer are many foreign brands: Adidas, Puma, Zara, Samsung, Louis

Vuitton, and LG Electronics. Whole rows of stores specialize in knockoff designer clothes. For instance, the brand didas with the "A" missing, and two instead of three stripes. You can also find Calven Kliem underwear, and Tommy Dooyao pants, with a logo very similar to Tommy Hilfiger, as well as pocket calculators from Cetezen and Casho. Customers interested in footwear apparently produced by the American company Columbia have to look even more carefully. While the original logo consists of eight rectangles forming a diamond, the local variant is a swastika.

"Kish is a tax-free zone; everything is 10 to 40 per cent cheaper here," says Masoud, pointing at the masses hustling and bustling in the amphitheater-sized inner hall. "As you can see the Iranians love shopping, especially the women."

And they love fast food, particularly the women. "If I want to eat traditional Iranian food, I cook it myself," says Mahbube 2, the pragmatic art student. For the evening meal at Iranwich there is Greek pizza and Pepsi served on white corrugated cardboard, on a wooden board. The restaurant looks like a large

47

McDonald's and is full to the last seat; we have to wait for a free table. The walls, chairs, and menu are all as red as the ketchup, which comes with every meal (Iranians always eat pizzas with ketchup). There is a cartoon on the TV screen with cute beavers and caterpillars. With immense effort and great persuasiveness I manage to win the debate about who pays for the pizzas. It is already 10 PM, and I am so hungry that I almost order two of the calorie bombs that are dripping in cheese and fat.

"Do you always eat at this time in the evening?" I ask Masoud.

"No, not always, Sometimes at eleven o'clock or midnight. A couple months ago I had a Swiss guest who always wanted to eat at six o'clock—crazy guy!"

Just as I was going to launch into a short lecture about mealtimes recommended by nutritionists, Masoud's phone rings. He holds a short conversation and then asks: "Do you want to go fishing now?"

I'm tired from the heat and worn out by the pizza, but I did promise myself to go along with even the not-so-good suggestions of my hosts. "Of course. I'd love to," I lie.

"Do you really have to?" asks Mahbube 2, reflecting my real thoughts. I get the feeling that she is not a big fan of his angling hobby. He, however, doesn't want her to keep him from it. They have been married five years.

From: Kian Qeshm
Hey Stephan! I'm kian from qeshm island. I'm really waiting to meet you. At the moment because of holidays I am in Tehran but on Friday I am going to go to my lovely island. See you soon Cheers

We take a cab home. Masoud prays briefly toward Mecca. Mecca is located opposite the TV. *Kolah Ghermezi*, red cap, a popular Persian puppet comedy series, is on. It appears to be as harmless as *Sesame Street*, but because of its implied social criticism it has few followers among the powerful. Mahbube 2 turns up the volume; the characters have penetrating high voices. Nine feet away Masoud prostrates himself and chants his *Allahu Akbars*.

I take a quick shower. One of the seldom expressed truths of couchsurfing is that, above all else, it is the activities that take place in the bathroom and all the associated collateral damage that can most easily sour relationships with hosts. Politeness, same wavelength, a particularly apt present—all for nothing when a guest blushingly announces that an emergency call to the plumber is required.

Nowhere else in a strange apartment lurk as many traps as in the bathroom. Idiosyncratic flushing devices, fittings that drop from walls, and rebellious shower heads/tap levers, just to mention a few of the harmless variations. Last year an Iranian host warned me on my arrival not to touch the warm water switch. There was something wrong with the cable, and within minutes a smoldering fire would result. (A thankfully never-posted online review: *Thanks for the accommodation. Sorry again that I torched your apartment complex. The pancakes at breakfast were delicious.*)

The differences in intercultural usage of toilets are also treacherous. In Iran squat toilets are standard, with a hose for cleaning purposes, which is usually on a small hook near the washbasin. Sometimes, next to it, there is a roll of toilet paper, sometimes not. Sometimes there's a small garbage can nearby, sometimes not. At the entrance there is always a pair of flip-flops available as the floors are mostly wet in quite a number of places. A sociologist should research the behavior of a hundred western European test persons in such a toilet, just to see how many variations they could come up with for using the few available objects.

In some countries the paper can be flushed away, in others it belongs in the garbage can. Elsewhere, both are wrong, and the routine is to leave as little used toilet paper as possible in places where people might potentially see it. Iran belongs to the last category, which is why the hose usage should be practiced every day until perfected, and less and less additional paper is necessary. Mastery has been reached when public toilets, the highest level of difficulty (dirty, no paper, stink level—ammonia synthesis reactor), can be approached reasonably fearlessly. In most of them there aren't even paper towels for the washbasins.

Maybe here I could mention a typical beginner's mistake. A German friend, on returning from a trip to Iran, remarked that Iranian toilets were ideal places to train thigh muscles. Now, if the Iranians, Chinese, and Indians hadn't learned, at the latest as three-year-olds, that the best method is to squat as low as possible, then they would all have thighs like weightlifters.

In Masoud's bathroom there are two challenges. First, there is only a tiny hook on the wall for towel and clothes. This is fairly common in most Iranian households, and it doesn't seem usual to hang anything in the bathroom except on the door handle. Second, the floor of the shower is level with the bathroom floor, so I unavoidably flood the bathroom, because the tiles are not sloped enough to channel the water into the toilet's drainage system.

Probably it would have been okay to leave the bathroom with a couple inches of water on the ground. But as a guest you always want to do things particularly well. Unfortunately, there is no available equipment for mopping up water. And that is why if someone had opened the door, they would have found the following scene: a clumsy foreigner on all fours, with a towel wrapped around his waist and wearing the right flip-flop, balancing the naked left foot on the narrow doorstep, trying to guide the water toward the drain with the left flip-flop. I think my new BDSM friends from Tehran would have found it all stunningly humiliating.

THE PERSIAN GULF

MASOUD AND I gather our jackets and a bite to eat, then go with Saler to the main road to wait for Masoud's "fishing buddy." I suddenly notice that I've forgotten my headlamp, and Masoud gives me the keys to the apartment. I walk back, knock briefly, and enter to find on the spotted sofa a strange woman, in jogging pants, very pretty, and with the opulent hairstyle of a 1970s soul singer. She looks shocked, and in a split second I realize that I'm looking at the unveiled version of Mahbube 2. She looks totally different. I quickly duck behind the door. "Come in," she says quickly, and I apologize profusely. She doesn't seem very happy, and I hope that, at least partially, it is because of our fishing trip and not just my stupid faux pas.

Masoud's friend Darius arrives somewhat late, with a backpack and fishing rod. He is roughly in his mid-fifties; has white hair, a white mustache, and black eyebrows; and can say *guten Tag* in German. We take a cab to the fishing port, driving to the end of a long pier. The man behind the steering wheel keeps asking whether this really is our destination. We climb over a few rocks, and Masoud and Darius prepare their rods.

"Bring a man a fish and you feed him for a day; teach a man to fish and you feed him for a lifetime," announces Masoud.

So he proceeds to teach me how to fish. Well, at least partly. My task for the night consists, after baiting the hook, of attaching a clasp with two small bells to the fishing rod. The ringing of the bells signals that the rod is bending significantly, indicating that a fish has probably fallen for the bait. Sometimes, however, a gust of wind is enough to create the sound.

While the two rods are jammed between rocks, and we wait for the jingling of bells, I ask Masoud where his perfect American accent comes from. "I'm a great fan of the American motivational speaker Anthony Robbins," he replies. "Once I searched for his name on Skype and actually found someone. Not the right one, but I still wrote to him. Now we are friends, and I've practiced a lot of English with him."

I've always understood night angling to be an activity where men keep the conversation to the essentials, contemplate the stars, the waves, life, and death, all while nipping at a hip flask every now and then. None of this applies to our first hours on the shore. Initially, I had considered Masoud to be not all that talkative, but now he opens up.

He tells of his half-hour online session that he booked with one of Anthony Robbins's assistants. "He asked me what my aim in life was, and I said I wanted to be a millionaire. He said: 'That's the wrong approach—simply formulating an aim. You have to focus on yourself first. Do you know any flight dispatchers or part-time English teachers who are millionaires? No. Then you have to change something in your life, found a company, for instance.'" Masoud already has an idea for a

53

business, and soon he is planning to move to Shiraz to set up a language café for Iranians and foreigners.

"And become a millionaire—with a café?" I ask.

"No, not with that. But it's all about having an aim in life. For example, my grandma is eighty-five and buys enough stock of some provisions for ten years. She will probably live that long simply because she is firmly convinced of it."

Masoud recommends some books to me: *Think and Grow Rich*,[1] *The 7 Habits of Highly Effective People: Powerful Lessons in Personal Change*,[2] and *Awaken the Giant Within: How to Take Immediate Control of Your Mental, Emotional, Physical and Financial Destiny!*[3] He has absorbed many of the principles described in them and uses them daily.

There is a sound of jingling, almost imperceptible against the noise of the breakers but unmistakable. Masoud grabs the rod and begins to reel it in. The line becomes taut, the rod parabolic; he purses his lips with the strain. On the surface a wild splashing of something-or-other can be seen, certainly longer than a couple feet. But then the rod springs back. "Damn it! It's escaped," curses Masoud. "Haven't got a clue what it was; something big. But that's what's great about fishing—you don't know what you've got until the last moment."

"Bit like couchsurfing," I add.

On the horizon are the lights of hotels and construction sites, and here, the lights of our headlamps. We nibble at some *tochme* (sunflower seeds), pistachios, and dry lemon cake. And that's the only nibbling that goes on for a number of hours. It's already 2:30 AM, and gradually I am the one who needs a motivational trainer to stop me suggesting that we give up and go to bed. But who needs a coach when you have Masoud?

"Mistakes are good, as they are the chance to learn something," he says, and we change position and go some 150 feet back toward the pier. A good decision, as within a few minutes the bells are jingling.

Darius reels in a roughly twenty-five-inch-long sea catfish. Saler stomps on it and hits it on the head with pliers until it stops floundering. A few minutes later Masoud gets lucky and after a short tug-of-war lands another catfish on the stones. Now we're in business!

By first light, a milky, blurry sunrise, we have caught four catfish, a Hamour (a kind of grouper), and a bream.

We walk a few minutes to the fish market nearby and have our catch filleted. The man is particularly rough with the catfish, deliberately cutting off large chunks and throwing the rest into a container outside as if disgusted with it. "Fish without scales are not halal according to Islam, and believers are not allowed to eat them," Masoud explains. The bag with filets he passes on to Darius; he's not such a strict observer.

After staying up all night and with just a few hours' sleep on the carpet, the best place to recover on Kish is to have a lazy day at the beach. After all, the island is supposed to have the prettiest beaches in Iran. Masoud has to work, so I travel alone to the northeast. I need caffeine, so I order a ZamZam cola, made in Iran, which tastes like Coca-Cola but with more sugar and less fizz. The moniker is interesting, as Zamzam is the name of a holy well in Mecca. A strange idea to give such a name to something as all-American as cola.

On the bike path girls pedal past on bikes with low-slung seats. Here girls don't have to worry about getting into trouble with the moral police. On Kish the regulations are more relaxed than elsewhere in the country. Female vacationers stroll barefoot on the beaches, wear sandals or skin-tight leggings. I even spot one without any head covering at all, which would be unthinkable in any other Iranian city. Motorboats pull rubber dinghies full of screaming tourists through the surf, a couple of girls and boys play beach soccer, and cameleers wait for customers. In a wooden pavilion a musician with a goatee finds a groove on his daf, a flat, round drum, but when a patrol car stops nearby he quickly packs away his instrument.

Sitting two tables away from me is a fifty-year-old lady with a light green hijab, a leopard-print silk scarf, and a huge silver wristwatch. She is listening to "Wind of Change," her cell phone resting against her sunglasses case so that the speaker is directed toward her ears. There is a bowl of chips, a pack of Kent cigarettes, and a plastic beaker of tea on the table. Klaus Meine sings about hope, about a better future. More bikes roll by, and the palms bow to the quite respectable breeze. Kish is well known for its winds. Catamarans are often forced to beach because of the choppy conditions.

Then we get talking. Her name is Afsaneh. She moved from Tehran to the island seven years ago.

"I love the fresh air, the sea, the relaxed atmosphere," she says. Twice a week she takes a walk to the beach. "I enjoy walking a lot—Tehran's too dirty, too much smog."

As if this were a keyword, she lights up a cigarette. Women aren't permitted to smoke in Iran. More "Wind of Change" emanates from her cell phone, words about the wind of change blowing into time's face, the same way a stormy wind would ring a bell of freedom, and I'd love to believe it. But Kish is hardly the moral laboratory for the future, rather a temporary place of escape, an isolated exclave of small freedoms, like a vacation with grandma and grandpa, where the kids can run wild and are allowed to eat more candy, but tougher rules apply as soon as they return to their parents.

So that the Iranians don't notice that the additional freedoms are the best thing about their Kish stay, there are shopping centers, motorboats, ghost trains, and a seventy-hectare amusement park, complete with a bird garden and a dolphinarium. I ask Afsaneh about the dolphins cleaning their teeth.

"Yes, it's true, and one dolphin can paint. The pictures cost between US$1,000 and US$8,000," she says.

Impulsively, I play with the idea of buying a dolphin. How much would you have to pay for such a creature?

"A million American dollars," she replies.

Okay, at an average of US$4,500 per painting, I would have almost redeemed my costs after two hundred paintings. I dismiss this business idea and buy myself an ice cream, instead.

Then I go and take a look at some world-famous soccer players. The road leading to the beach is flanked by larger-than-life plastic caricatures. The FIFA World Cup is soon to begin, and Iran has qualified for the first time in many years. Messi and Neymar have a lot of hair and little face. The athlete marked Mesut Özil, however, with a small tuft of hair, a gigantic nose, and huge bulging eyes, resembles something you might encounter during an excursion in a glass-bottom boat. Maybe the dolphins painted him.

. . . .

THE NEXT MORNING I'm awoken by Pitbull and Masoud, a marriage made in hell. My place to crash was on the carpet directly beneath the TV, and at 7:30 AM my host has the brilliant idea of playing a music video of the American rapper at nightclub volume. Like an aerobic trainer with ADHD he dances through the apartment, singing along to Pitbull's "Rain over Me" at the top of his voice. With that din you could probably raise the dead— and a sleeping tourist, for sure. In the clip a BMW Z4 hurtles through a desert landscape with more than a little likeness to Kish.

"It's time for breakfast and Nature Day!" Masoud bellows cheerfully. In contrast to me, Masoud is obviously a morning person. By "Nature Day" he means *Sizdah Be-dar*, the conclusion of the two-week *Nowruz* festivities, an Iranian public holiday when everybody spends the day outdoors and picnics.

Mahbube 1 and 2 quickly spread a plastic sheet on the floor and deck it with pita bread, goat cheese, and homemade carrot jam. After a quick breakfast we fill the picnic hamper with a few items from the fridge and go down to the street to find a cab. A Toyota instead of a Z4 roadster, but the driver knows a thing or two about racing. We stop at a section of the shore with a rocky beach and wooden pavilions with solar panels on the roof—they are already occupied; we are too late. So we spread our picnic rug on a stretch of sand, and Masoud places a few pieces of chicken with a saffron-lemon marinade on the grill belonging to the nearest pavilion.

Children are the best language teachers in the world. I get involved in a game of pointing to objects and naming them in Persian and English with Saler and Saba. The kids enjoy it so much that they don't want to stop. We repeat the terms until I can say: sea (*daryâ*), sky (*asemân*), cloud (*âbr*), fish (*mâhi*), sun (*chorschid*), apple (*sib*), ear (*gosch*), nose (*bini*), eye (*tscheschm*), and auto (*mâschin*). Our strolling along the shore does Saler's language skills some good, as up until now his English repertoire has only consisted of the perfectly pronounced "How are you?" and "Get out of my face, asshole!"

Exactly a year ago, on my first trip to Iran, I also celebrated Nature Day, but with Yasmin and her family. Roughly fifty people had gathered together in a garden surrounded by high walls outside Tehran. We played volleyball and danced forbidden dances to Persian pop music, and inside the house there was whiskey. The streets outside the capital were completely covered by picnic blankets and tents—every piece of derelict land became an outdoor feasting area. When 30 or 50 or even 60 million people leave their secure homes and party just for one day, a state of emergency reigns in Iran.

I was expecting a greater degree of excess on the paradise island of Kish than in Tehran, but Masoud has to work, as airplanes also fly on public holidays. So, we nibble at our saffron chicken, look at the waves, and pack everything together just after midday and head home.

My time on Kish is coming to an end. On my last evening, star chef Mahbube 2 prepares another feast: self-caught bream and grouper with rice.

LOST IN TRANSPORTATION I

THE POPULAR TRAVELER'S game of ticket window ping-pong
goes as follows: the tourist (mostly equipped with a heavy
backpack and minimal language skills) tries to mime his wish
to buy a ticket for a bus or train, a ship, or a plane and is sent
somewhere else. On reaching this place he/she is directed
somewhere else, where he/she is again passed on to someone
else. This can take up a fair amount of time, but not an eternity,
as no terminal in the world has an endless number of ticket
windows.

When all the legwork is over, and the tourist has a ticket in
his hand and can depart, he wins. As soon as a contact point
is mentioned for the second time, he loses. Continuous loop,
game over. Variations of this game can be found in tax offices
and telephone hotlines of Internet providers.

My round begins at the entrance to the futuristic boat terminal, where the cab driver dropped me. A little man in a blue
uniform points to the right: "Old terminal," he says.

I walk five hundred feet to the right, where a soldier uncom-prehendingly shrugs his shoulders and points to two wooden huts, one blue and the other red, which can be seen some six hundred feet way. According to the pictures next to the sales windows, it's small boats to the left and large boats to the right. The left side of the counter is closed, so I join the line to the right window, where six people are already in the line. Judging by the length of time they spend at the window, they appear to be paying for their tickets by giving an extensive update on the state of health of their extended families. After what feels like an eternity it's my turn.

"You cannot get ticket now," says the ticket seller. In my defense I tell him that I was sent here.

"No. Passport first, passport," he says, pointing toward the terminal from which I had come.

Damn it! Third contact point, ping-pong game over. But I don't give up so quickly. Back to the soldier. "Passport, pass-port," I say, while waving it around. On my surprise return he looks at me as if I were an alien, hunching his shoulders even more than the first time. He points to the two wooden huts behind me. Both of us spend the next few moments thinking about how stupid the other person is.

Suddenly, out of nowhere, a chubby port employee appears from the darkness of the old terminal.

"Mister, come here." He leads me to an office, where there are two other men in shirts and suit pants, one of whom fetches me a glass of water. "Passport, please. Where do you come from? Are you enjoying yourself in Iran? Sit down. Would you like a tea? Where do you want to go?"

"Germany." "Very much." "Yes, please." "Charak," I reply. That is the nearest town on the mainland, and according to the guidebook, a roughly forty-minute boat trip.

"And where are you going after that?"

"Bandar Abbas." About four hours from Charak by bus.

"A big ship is going to Bandar Lengeh in three hours; it's nearer than Bandar Abbas," he says.

"How long does it take?"

"Four hours. And from there it's two hours to Bandar Abbas."

"Then it's still quicker to go via Charak. Is anything heading there soon?"

"I don't know."

One of his colleagues is better informed. "Charak now," he says, taking my passport from the photocopying machine and beckoning me to follow him. He walks briskly through the hall to the quay just in time to see a sailor releasing the bow rope. The small ship chugs off so slowly that with a spirited jump I might just about have caught it. The colleague waves and shouts, but the boat doesn't turn back.

So, back to the new terminal, which is ninety feet high and finely decorated in silver, gray, and beige. Flat-panel displays show advertising spots for condos and tourist attractions, for the ancient city of Harireh, Underwater World, and a horse race. I have missed most of the attractions on the island, but the hours spent with Masoud and his wonderful family were better than any dolphin park.

The waiting room is full of passengers, and the detour via the quay meant that I bypassed all the security controls.

"The next ship to Charak departs in twenty-five minutes," says my helper before disappearing, never to be seen again. All the other passengers are holding tickets in their hands, but I still don't have one. Eventually, the departure for Charak is announced, a line forms in front of the ticket control at the exit to the quay, and, sure enough, I'm able to pay cash there— 27,000 toman, which is around seven dollars. I don't get a ticket for it, though. The employee just pockets the money and waves me through.

No ticket, one double visit to a contact point, and I still reach my destination. This bout of ticket window ping-pong is mine.

From: Kian Qeshm

Good morning Today I will arrive qeshm at 3 p.m. Unfortunately because I live in company's accommodation I can't host but maybe we can meet.

ARYANS

IN CONTRAST TO the terminal, the *Pelican* is anything but futuristic. Tatty upholstery, threadbare Persian carpets, and a motor that sounds like a dying jackhammer. Just as I'm wondering whether it will make the twelve miles to the shore before giving up the ghost, as if on cue, the motor chokes. An angry-looking giant tries to heave his heavyweight-boxer body up the steel ladder to the bridge. His two companions are luckily (a) of a similar bouncer-like stature and (b) of the opinion that beating up the captain will not relieve the technological problems. With a united effort they manage to hold him back.

"Arabs," says my neighbor scornfully. He, too, is well-built. In comparison, my shoulders seem meager and my biceps modest. "*Alamâni*: high; *Irani*: high; Arabs: low," he declares in broken English. I had already told him that I was German. He points, first to me and then himself, and says "Aryans," then plumps his thigh-sized upper arm round my shoulders.

Within a second I can think of three hundred reasons for which I would rather be liked. But the Aryan topic is a big thing in Iran, and even the country's name is derived from Aryan. Here the word isn't associated with racist ideologies and the Holocaust but used as naturally as if you were calling a Chinese person an Asian, or a Croat a Slav. Thousands of years before dubious European scientists thought up attributes like blond, blue-eyed, and Nordic type, the Iranians were already known as Aryans. To this day they are convinced that they share a heritage with Germanic and Indian peoples, which is why they are the only country in the world where Germans are still respected as Aryans.

After a ten-minute break the motor indignantly splutters to life, and the decrepit *Pelican* renews efforts to reach the gray cliffs of the mainland. My neighbor introduces himself as Nader. He comes from Kerman. His two friends with almost identical T-shirts bearing a huge *Abercrombie & Fitch* print, one in gray and the other in white, are Moshtaba from Bandar Abbas and Ismail from Isfahan. All three are wearing very new sport shoes and have very new cell phones in their hands. None of them speaks English well, which is why I use the best small-talk-despite-language-barrier trick in the world and change the subject from ethnology to soccer. A verbatim transcript could never do justice to the emotional intensity of the conversation. It goes something like this:

"Mehdi Mahdavikia!"

"Ooh, good!"

"Ali Daei!"

"Ali Daei! Bayern Munich good! Schwains-Tiger! Ballack! Lahm!"

"Yes, very good players!"

"World Cup! Brazil!"

"Iran against Argentina, ooh!"

"Messi! Ooooh no!"

After this exchange we are best friends. The three guys
ask whether I need a lift to Bandar Abbas. The ship docks at
Charak, and soon we are sitting in Ismail's age-worn white
Peugeot. We crunch away at nuts, listen to the Gypsy Kings
and hurtle eastward. Foam dice swing back and forth beneath
the rearview mirror.

There is a strong resemblance between traveling and a
game of dice. Had I caught an earlier ship, or sat somewhere
else once on board, I wouldn't be sitting in this car. In Tehran,
if I hadn't contacted Yasmin but one of the thousand other
potential hosts, I wouldn't soon be visiting the battlefields on
the Iraqi border.

From the window a shimmering desert landscape flashes by,
with wind-formed sand dunes and signposts warning of cam-
els. Conical cisterns look like the tips of buried stone rockets.
Having done soccer players, other sports stars become our next
topic. "Ismail Schumacher," says Nader, grinning and pointing
at his friend behind the wheel, who drives as if Mika Häkkinen
and Damon Hill are in hot pursuit.

The racer poses would be perfect, were he not a chain-
smoker and therefore only has one hand permanently on the
steering wheel. At two of the speed bumps our car almost
takes off, with the consequence that at the next bump our
driver is more cautious, braking directly beforehand and causing our suspension to screech. I know no other country with
so many speed bumps. Iran is speed-bump country, and I'm
sure that's a metaphor for something.

Recently, a statistic was published claiming that 25,000 had
died in the previous year in traffic accidents; that is 68 a day.
The government now aims to reduce the number to 20,000.

At any rate, gas prices don't deter people from speeding. We fill up for 140 rial per gallon, which is all of twenty cents. At the halfway mark we stop at a beach to drink tea with hot water from a thermos. I drink it without sugar, which earns me three puzzled looks.

Nader looks miserably at his tea bag. The tag reads *Ahmad Tea London.* "English bad!" he says, crossing both index fingers. "English against Iran." The British had made a killing with Iranian gas and oil in the first half of the twentieth century by duping the shah into exploitative contracts. I feel Nader's hand on my shoulder. "Hitler good. Hitler help Iran." Hitler never wanted oil from Persia in the Second World War because they were allies. This is turning into quite a challenging conversation, given our language barrier.

I babble in broken English: "Hitler not good!"

He asks: "Merkel good?"

I deliberate briefly before saying: "Hitler bad, Merkel good," which admittedly is a gross simplification but, in this comparison, not wrong. The rest of the journey we don't speak much, but I wish that I could say more in Persian than fish and sun.

In the port city of Bandar Abbas we say our goodbyes, and I catch a boat that is twice as big and three times as modern as the *Pelican* to the island of Qeshm. I had hoped to have a host there, but Kian had texted me to say that unfortunately his apartment belongs to his company, and they don't allow visitors.

To: Kian Qeshm   67
Hey Kian, no problem, would be great to meet! Can you recommend a hotel to stay?

From: Kian Qeshm
Ask the taxi driver for Hafez guesthouse, its not expensive
but I m not sure if it's clean

From an open deck I view the huge oil and gas tankers of
the Persian Gulf. Many are old and barely seaworthy. It's difficult to see whether they are moving without looking for the
anchor line in the water. The whims of traveler's dice have
placed a family behind me with a daughter who I guess to be
about twenty and two sons, maybe six and eight. The younger
son is staring at me with huge dark brown eyes. I leaf through
my Persian phrasebook and read the sentence "*Esme tan tschi
ast?*"—What's your name? The parents are named Reza and
Ehsan, the girl, Mobina, and the family comes from a place near
Yazd. The rest of the conversation consists of "Welcome to
Iran" and "Do you like Iran?" And, above all, plenty of friendly
and curious looks. Mobina asks for my cell phone number. We
wish each other a good time on the island, she takes a picture
of me, and we go our separate ways.

A cab driver, in a prehistoric Toyota Corolla, drives through
featureless streets with endless rows of stores to the Hafez
Guesthouse. On telling him about my home country he
stretches out his right hand and screams, "Heil Hitler!" and
laughs amicably. Somehow today's jinxed.

THE GENIE

A<small>T THE ENTRANCE</small> to the Hafez Guesthouse a few teenagers are hanging out. As I enter they seem amused that at last something is happening there. Using sign language, I communicate to a young man behind the counter in a Barcelona soccer shirt that I'm looking for a room. He looks at me somewhat quizzically.

"Double room forty thousand, no single room," says a man without a single hair on his head but an abundant growth on his chest that couldn't be missed, as he is only wearing scruffy track pants and sandals. He, too, is only a guest, which doesn't deter him from going through the check-in formalities.

"Don't eat here; the food's no good," he adds. But the rooms are safe. Mine is exactly as wide as two beds, and I don't need a tape measure to establish this, as there are two beds placed next to each other, on top of which are two stained bed covers with Cinderella motifs. A tube, looking as if it were made shortly after the Industrial Revolution, runs from the air conditioner through the middle of a frosted glass pane to the outside. Someone seems to have used a hammer to make the necessary hole for the tube, and at one point the gap is so big that it allows a single shaft of sunlight to enter the room. The metal double doors to the hall also have a window, which has been covered by a poster advertising *Deluxe Diamond* T-shirts. There is precious little else deluxe here. The furnishings consist of a tiny CRT TV (broken), a Super General fridge (loud), and a blotchy carpet.

After a few minutes, someone knocks at the door. The bald-headed guest again, whose sudden appearance reminds me of a good-natured genie in a bottle. He hands me a hotel business card, on which he has written his name, *Mehran*, and his cell phone number. "If you need help, give me a call." Maybe it's not as safe here as I thought.

He then shows me the washroom, which can only be reached via a small courtyard. The light doesn't work in the men's shower. "You can use the women's shower in the morning," he says.

"Would you like a drink," he asks. "I have some Iranian vodka. Absolutely forbidden!" He signals for me to follow him and explains how he got the stuff. "I combed all the pharmacies and said I needed ethyl alcohol for insect bites." After a few attempts he was successful; the assistant asked him whether he wanted a large or small bottle. Small, he said, so as not to raise suspicions, and then inquired about the price. Of course, the larger ones were cheaper. He pretended to ponder the options before deciding to take the larger bottle. Twenty thousand toman, five dollars. "That's what I always do. Come in."

He opens the door to his room; it has the same prison-cell dimensions as mine. A small boy is sleeping on the bed. From the floor next to the fridge, Mehran picks up a heavy two-pint flask with a round belly and short neck that wouldn't have looked out of place in an apothecary museum. *Ethyl Alcohol 96%* is written on the label next to *Highly Flammable*. The amount would be enough for quite a number of insect bites. "We can mix it with water or Pepsi," says Mehran. "At home in Tehran I drink a bottle in five days. Don't worry, you won't be arrested. This stuff is good. After all, it comes from the pharmacist— medical quality."

The term brings back memories; I remember it from last year's trip. "Medical quality," said the student Samira from Tabriz as she fetched a bottle of ethanol from a cupboard almost exactly a year ago. Alcohol content 70 per cent, a demon's drink. Mixed with orange juice it still tasted like hard candy dissolved in gasoline. We lay on a rug on the floor of her student digs and watched *The Exorcist* on a laptop. Three long days we traveled through the wilds of Kurdistan, getting drunk on long drinks from hell and smoking melon-flavored shisha. We spoke much of freedom, which meant we spoke of the chances for her to leave the country.

Of course, I wanted to meet up with her again, but a couple weeks ago she contacted me to say that she had made it.

Samira is now studying engineering in Shanghai on a scholarship and doesn't plan to return.

Taste and smell are more deeply embedded in memory than experiences. Memories of the hard-candy taste flood back, and I even believe I can feel a slight rasping in my throat. And anyway, the experiences connected to the memories weren't that good, so I turn down ethanol and cola or ethanol soda or whatever else Mehran is planning to serve up today.

The next morning the light in the washroom still isn't working, so I creep off to the women's unit. What on earth happens in Iran if you are caught in the women's washroom? I think I would have simply said that the genie in the bottle sent me there.

Couchsurfer Kian can only meet me in the evening, so I explore the island with a cab driver. Qeshm is notorious for its smugglers, who transport cigarettes and gas canisters to the Musandam Peninsula or to the United Arab Emirates in wooden boats. But it is also famous for its canyons and sandstone mesas, which you would think you were more likely to see in Utah as the backdrop to a cowboy movie. Apart from that, plenty of dust, a couple of chimneys burning gas, and mangrove wood on the shore. Unlike the fifteen-times-smaller Kish, Qeshm isn't geared toward mass tourism.

But, as Kian explains over an evening meal of fish stew in an austere restaurant with wobbly tables and designer lamps, that is all about to change. He is a pleasantly chubby guy, 6'2", red Nike polo shirt, and rimless glasses. Two new five-star hotels are being constructed, as well as four shopping centers, he explains. As far as hotels are concerned, in my mind there's room indeed for improvement. The state is creating the prerequisites for the boom—contractors pay no taxes, the same

72

applies for employees like Kian, who works as an engineer for a gas power plant.

He tells me that today is an important day for Iran. As part of the nuclear negotiations, sanctions against Iran have been relaxed. From today, for the first time in thirty-five years, airplane parts can be imported from the U.S. On top of that, Iran can again export oil, and 4.9 billion of a total 100 billion U.S. dollars frozen in foreign accounts has been released. "We have had two hundred plane accidents in recent decades, with more than two thousand deaths, which were mostly down to the lack of spare parts," explains Kian. Supplies of medication have also been affected by the sanctions and caused many deaths in Iran, among cancer patients, for instance. "It never hurts the government but always the ordinary people."

In the summer Kian plans to travel to Europe. First to Italy, because he's heard that it's the easiest place to get Schengen visas. From there to Disneyland, near Paris, then to Germany, where an uncle lives near Stuttgart. His uncle has already taught him three words, which he proudly recites: *"tschüss"* (bye) and *"guts nächtle"* (good night in the Swabian dialect).

LOST IN
TRANSPORTATION II

THE NEXT MORNING I take the ferry back to the mainland. In the bleak bus terminal of Bandar Abbas I ping-pong from counter to counter until eventually a giggling woman in a chador sells me a ticket to Bam. She asks for my passport so that she can enter my name on the ticket. While I'm rummaging through my backpack, she has second thoughts and simply writes "Mr. Price" on my ticket. Allah only knows how she chose that name. From the poster on the wall behind the counter, Ayatollah Khomeini looks down on me probingly.

I have an hour to kill before departure, so I buy myself a kebab: burnt chicken bits, black-red tomatoes, and onions in pita bread.

"Where do you come from?" asks the vendor.

"Germany," I reply.

"Alamâni! Germany, Aryan! Klinsmann!" he says

"Ali Daei! Mehdi Mahdavikia!" I reply.

Soccer Esperanto always works. We both laugh, but I feel a bit like a dumbass everybody is nice to because they all think that the poor old guy hasn't got it easy in life, so we may as well be friendly to him. It's high time I learned Persian.

Of course, with these thoughts I'm being unfair to the cheerful vendor. But everyone who travels extensively knows you make a fool of yourself three to ten times more often when you're away from home. Buying fruit, at the ticket window, asking for directions. When routine situations that at home come naturally suddenly require a creative solution, then it's a good experience because it teaches you humility and to laugh at yourself. You can be a five-year-old child again on a dare buying a strawberry ice cream with your mom's money. Simple exercises, with failure and tears not excluded. Sometimes at an interview they ask applicants more personal questions, such as: When did you last push yourself to your limits? I think it would be much more revealing to know when someone last made a complete and utter fool of themselves.

Possible answer: while looking for the right bus at the huge bus terminal at Bandar Abbas. The fact that I'm having difficulties is mostly to do with the name of my intended destination. I approach a driver and a porter and ask: "Bam?" and they reply, "Bam!" and "Bam!" and nod and point and take me by the hand, and soon I'm sitting in a blue bus, the Bam bus. Allah is written on the back and Adidas on the sides, so you can choose your God.

Bam doesn't seem to be a particularly popular destination. Apart from Mr. Price from Germany there are five other passengers on board. They are all wearing loose-fitting white smocks and wide pants, and they look more Pakistani than Iranian.

The farther the bus travels north, the greener the landscape and the higher the surrounding mountains. Palm trees and greenhouses line the road, and many fuel tankers are traveling today. I read my phrase book and murmur Persian sentences. My cell phone rings. Unknown number with a 0098 code, so it's Iranian. The reception here is terrible—a female voice, but I don't understand a single word. At some stage I imagine that I might have heard "I love you!" but it was probably just the wishful thinking of a lonely bus passenger on a hot, sultry day of travel. Busy signal. Then a couple more calls from the same number, but as soon as I answer the caller hangs up.

At a police checkpoint a soldier with a bulletproof vest and machine gun gets on the bus. He ignores all the other guests, but he asks me for my passport and signals me to follow him. On a platform between the barriers separating the traffic lanes, the crushed remains of a wrecked car are displayed like a piece of art. There's hardly anything left of the hood, the windscreen and other windows are all smashed, and parts of the chassis are burnt black. The vehicle must have crashed against an obstacle at high speed. Now it is being used as a warning to other speedsters, a metallic equivalent to the pictures of lung cancer patients on packs of cigarettes. The soldier, watched by two curious colleagues, leafs through the visas of a number of countries that I've visited. Apparently he's fascinated by how much I've been getting around.

"China?"

"Yes, *kheili khub*," I say—very pretty.

"Nepal?"

"*Kheili khub.*"

"Ghana?"

"*Kheili khub.*"

He hands back my passport and wishes me bon voyage. I've survived my first official questioning. On the way back to my seat I feel the looks of my fellow passengers. The driver puts his foot down, but half an hour later the bus stops again. A couple of swashbuckling guys with beards and long hair embark. Strangely enough, apart from small handbag-sized bundles, they don't appear to have any luggage, although it's still hundreds of miles to the bus destination, Zahedan, on the Pakistan border.

From: Number Unknown
Hello, where is you? I want. Telphon nambr almani please you calling now. I am mobina

To: Mobina
Hi mobina, i m on a bus to bam, tomorrow kerman. Are you still on qeshm? Have a nice day!

I had almost forgotten about Mobina, the girl on the ferry trip to Qeshm. Her number, however, is different to the earlier one, where the phone call came from.

From: Mobina
Yes. I have a nice day. Can you speak pershin? I want tell phone.almani you
Shafa please.cam yazd

It's not too easy to guess what she wants. Okay, first of all: stay polite, somewhat distant, noncommittal but not unfriendly.

77

To: Mobina
Sorry i dont speak persian. I dont use almani phone now. I
will go to yazd in 3 days

Another phone call from the same number as before. The
thought of a laid-back backpacker slouching around in a bus
seems to have a magnetic effect on the ladies, but come to
think of it, the ladies can't even see me. This time the lady at
the other end of the line doesn't hang up. Again, I think I hear
"I love you" and "Where are you?" I break the connection after
two minutes because of the interfering noises and send a text
message.

To: Unknown Female Caller
Hi, how do i know you? I m traveling to bam and kerman now

From: Unknown Female Caller
Hi. Iammina.myfriendseeyouinbander.iamiran. plese come
hear Harat.icannotmanyspeakenqlish

She seems to have an extreme aversion to spaces. The only
people I met in "bander"—so, Bandar Abbas—were Ismail
Schumacher and the Hitler friends (which actually sounds
like a pretty crappy band name). Strange. But her "I am Iran"
appeals to me so much that I store the number under "Iran."

From: Iran
ILoveyou. Whataboutyou?

Anyone have any more questions about the laid-back bus
slouching poses? Iran loves me, although she hardly knows me.

Now, no mistakes. Keep a cool head. I wait half an hour before texting back. Not too emotional with the answer but also not too cool. Bear in mind the absurdity and the playfulness of the situation. Whatever you do, don't leave the impression that you're easy game.

To: Iran
I think i love you too

In the meantime it's become dark outside. The signpost reads *Abareq*, and a second sign says that Bam is twenty-four miles away. The bus slows down, turns into a side street, then a small parking area, where the driver maneuvers it back and forth until it is correctly parked. The driver turns off the motor and the lights; it is pitch black and silent.

In such situations I've become accustomed to carefully observing the reactions of the local travelers before getting nervous. No one's swearing, no discussions with the driver, no one seems surprised. There doesn't seem to be any cause for alarm. After a few minutes, a pickup with two spotlights and a large tank on its bed draws up and stops next to the bus.

The man who gets out looks like an Afghani version of Johnny Depp in *Pirates of the Caribbean* but with a turban instead of a pirate's tricorn hat and looking even more gaunt. At a casting session for an al-Qaeda movie he would have been guided to the front of the line, just out of fear that he might turn nasty. He rummages around a bit behind the bus, and it smells of gas. Okay, so we're refueling. It does seem to be taking a while, though—twenty minutes, thirty minutes. Still, no one seems surprised or alarmed.

79

I go outside to take a leak. Some of the passengers are sitting in a circle on the ground, smoking and waiting. Some men are wandering around with headlamps. Next to the bus there is a wooden crate containing rusty old tanks, a kind of pump, and some thick pipes. I almost bump into "Johnny Depp," who says, "*Chetori?*" (How are you?), to which I reply, "*Khubam*" (Fine), which isn't quite true because, according to the timetable, I should have reached my destination three hours ago. Then he continues fiddling around with his pipes.

It takes an hour until finally the motor starts and the lights are switched on. The bus interior stinks so pungently of gas that two women clasp their veils to their noses. The signposts show *Bam 9 miles* and *Bam 3 miles*. Everything was going too slowly before, and now everything is happening too fast. The bus fails to stop, although I told the driver my destination before we started. So, up to the front I go.

"Bam?" I inquire.

"Bam!" says the man behind the wheel, while making a semicircle sign with his hand, which, due to his relaxed tone of voice, I interpret as he will use the next opportunity to turn back. But in the ensuing minutes he stubbornly continues to drive straight on. I try to make him realize that I have to go to Bam, and he points backward. He chats a bit with his co-driver. Both seem to be inappropriately cheerful and not in the slightest affected by my fate.

The security advice of the State Department states that there is a "serious risk of kidnapping" in the east of Kerman Province and its neighboring province Sistan and Baluchestan. Even before my departure, I pondered just how far I would go to get my story of Iran. I decided to risk trouble with the authorities up to a certain point but to be overcautious as far as the dangers of kidnapping were concerned.

I say: "Stop here, please." No reaction. I try to remember where the next scheduled stop is. We are about to cross the Dasht-e-Lut Desert, and the next large town is Zahedan, 150 miles away.

At last the bus slows down and stops. The door opens, and the driver points to a restaurant on the opposite side of the road. His co-driver fetches my backpack from the luggage compartment.

I'm exhausted. I have a headache from the gas fumes and have been on the go for ten hours instead of six. Slowly, I trudge toward the restaurant. All I want now is a bed and some peace and quiet. I open the door. And then: streamers, tin whistles, balloons, paper hats, and "For He's a Jolly Good Fellow." "All just a bit of fun, Mr. Price. Ha-ha-ha, dumb name, ha-ha-ha," as the TV show presenter from *Candid Camera* emerges from the kitchen and points at a hidden camera next to the Ayatollah Khomeini poster.

That at least is how I felt on experiencing the sudden change in atmosphere. From the moment I cross the threshold I am surrounded by people who want to snap souvenir photos, welcome me, question me about my state of health, Iran, Europe, and the whole wide world. I am more interested in how to get to Bam, as it is almost midnight. But okay, first of all, sit down, drink a Hoffenberg lemon malt beer on the house. Welcome to Iran. More group photos, more good wishes.

And eventually a bus emerges from the darkness that really does go to Bam. It, too, smells as if someone has spilled a couple of canisters of diesel in the aisle. But that doesn't worry me anymore; it drops me at my destination, and I don't even have to pay.

EARTHQUAKES

"O H, SO YOU have been on one of the stinky busses," says Akbar Panjali jovially, as he places a late-night plate of rice and chicken in front of me. "They are diesel smugglers; they put tanks where the luggage usually goes, even under the seats. They can carry up to five hundred gallons." In Pakistan they pay seven times the price for Iranian diesel, and there have been no strict controls up to now. Business also flourishes in the other direction. In Bandar Abbas goods are smuggled in from the Gulf states. The villages around Bam are well situated as fueling stops for smugglers, as they are roughly halfway between the coast and the border.

"At the border you can see how the bus drivers quickly drop in on the police chief to deposit a couple million rials there," says Akbar. "Many of the passengers aren't even travelers, but accomplices." A couple weeks prior to my episode, an Iranian smuggler bus crashed into a truck in Pakistan. A huge fireball and thirty-eight deaths. But criminals are willing to run the risk of traveling hundreds of miles on a bomb on wheels because it is still considerably safer for them to earn money from fuel than heroin or opium. Iran's border guards act with utmost severity against the transport of drugs. The death penalty awaits those arrested, which is why there are often gun battles at the border.

Akbar is seventy-one, a cheerful soul with laugh lines and unkempt hair. He studied Persian literature and worked as an English teacher, which is why everyone here refers to him as "Akbar English." Nowadays, he runs Akbar's Tourist Guesthouse. The Colosseum, the Eiffel Tower, and the Leaning Tower of Pisa are pictured on his sign outside, which seems a strange choice of inducement, considering one of Iran's most famous monuments is only a couple minutes away by foot.

I contacted two couchsurfing members in Bam, but neither replied. You always need a Plan B when looking for places to stay for nothing, and Akbar was a very good Plan B. I feel this every time he says, "You're veeery welcome," extending the "e" almost excruciatingly. He's been officially providing rooms for sixteen years, previously offering them on the quiet and relying on word of mouth recommendations, as he had no

83

license. "Now I'm famous," he announces. "It helps being in the guidebooks."

At the moment, his fame doesn't seem to be helping him much. I am the only guest, and the place seems to be half construction site, with the rest pretty run-down. "In earlier days, 70 per cent of my guests were car and motorbike tourists on their way to India, but there have been problems with Pakistan over the last couple of years, and not so many people pass by these days," he adds.

I inquire whether it might have something to do with the dangers of kidnapping. "Bad things can happen everywhere, even in Hamburg or London," he replies. People who run hostels in this part of Iran need to have a more relaxed relationship to danger than someone in, say, Normandy or New Hampshire. Akbar tells me that the last kidnapping, a Japanese man, took place three years ago. "They held him for a month, and I will never forget what he said on release: 'I had a great time. There were endless supplies of hashish for nothing.'"

To: Hussein Kerman
Hi Hussein, how are you? Would it be possible to host me from tomorrow for one or two night? Would be great!

From: Hussein Kerman
Yes you can sleep, no problem

From: Mobina
Hi. Where is you? Please cam citi Harat. When cam back to alman?

To: Mobina
I will be in yazd in a few days. Where exactly is Harat?

From: Laila Hamburg
Hun! Hurraaaaah, just a couple of days now! How's the trip
been? See you very soon in Yazd!

Maybe the fears of tourists have so little effect on Akbar
because he already has experience with an apocalypse. Because
there was one event in his life that changed everything forever
and split his life in two, into a Before and an After. Deep below
the bed, with its somewhat hard mattress, on which I am now
spending the night, the Arabian Plate is forced beneath the
Eurasian Plate. On December 26, 2003, at 5:28 AM, there was
so much pressure that the ground shook—6.5 on the Richter
scale, a catastrophe that happens once a century. More than
26,000 people died in twelve seconds when half the city was
flattened.

"Luckily, I was at my parents' house, ten minutes away from
here, when it happened," says Akbar. Otherwise, he might
have been killed, his Akbar Tourist Guesthouse collapsed. Two
guests and his son's best friend died in the rubble.

Even today, more than thirteen years later, traces of the
tragedy in Bam cannot be missed. Not only in my accommodation, where renovation work is still incomplete. In the middle
of town there are still the ruins of a mosque. Some rows of
houses are broken by heaps of rubble, and in the ancient bazaar
there are piles of debris, while the remaining bazaar units are
still bare.

But the true memorial is the historical center with the citadel, Arg-e Bam, the largest adobe building in the world. Most

85

of its light brown walls and watchtowers had withstood all kinds of weathers and battles for more than a thousand years, until an earthquake destroyed one of Iran's greatest tourist attractions.

On a tour of its walls, which appear to have been made from compressed straw, you get the impression that the catastrophe not only robbed the city of its citadel walls but also of its soul. Despite this, it is a phenomenal location on the edge of a desert, where the midday heat with no shade can finish you off, and the dust leaves you clutching your throat. On the horizon, the snow-laden peaks of the thirteen-thousand-foot mountains loom.

Many buildings have already been restored. But even today, constructors clamber over the distinctive wooden scaffolding. The UNESCO World Heritage Foundation is helping finance the reconstruction. But this mixture of spotless reconstruction and total chaos, although impressive enough in its dimensions, fails to solve other problems. When you look at the pictures showing the same locations before the earthquake in the evening light, as romantic as *One Thousand and One Nights*, you cannot help feeling melancholic. There is a hushed atmosphere about the historical center of Bam, like a cemetery, with only the hammering of the laborers and the buzzing of flies breaking the silence.

ART

TRAVELING TO FAR-FLUNG places is the status symbol of my generation. In the olden days you used to park your sports car in front of the garage to make the neighbors envious. Today you can achieve this with a six-month backpacking tour of India or a trip through New Zealand in a vw motorhome. Among experienced travelers, however, there is a ranking in the destinations thats affects the amount of admiration and attention you receive on reporting your adventures. A solo tour of Iran is, at the moment, pretty high on the list and gets you more credit than, for instance, Albania, Mozambique, or Cuba and roughly the same as North Korea or Tibet. Only war-torn regions and countries with travel warnings—places like Afghanistan, Yemen, Syria, Somalia—can trump the prestige of an account of backpacker haunts in Iran.

But traveling here is relatively tolerable. The roads are well signposted, and buses are usually punctual (with the notable exception of smuggler buses). You can travel from A to B with fewer problems than in many Asian or South American countries. The locals, too, are willing to help as soon as they see someone in a public place standing around or seeming to be a bit lost.

The afternoon journey to Kerman in a savari, a shared taxi that takes a specified route as soon as there are four or five passengers, takes two hours. It is a little more expensive than the bus but much quicker and more comfortable. So much quicker that I arrive an hour before my planned meeting with Hussein, who is still at work. I put down my backpack and settle on a park bench in Tohid Square. In front of me is the entrance to the bazaar of the city with a population of 700,000 and a monument that looks something like an eighty-foot staple made of marble.

From: Iran
Tomorrow come here in yazd. Harat

Finally the penny drops. "Iran" and Mobina belong together; they come from the same place—Harat. So Mobina from the ferry was meant by "my friend in Bander," not one of the three Nazis. According to the map, Harat is some seventy-five miles from Yazd and not too far off my planned route to Shiraz. Might be worth considering. Not because I feel flattered and I'm getting silly ideas because of a flirty text message, but because I intend to keep my promise to myself about being flexible to other suggestions when traveling. Flattered? Nonsense! But how do I explain this to Laila?

To: Laila Hamburg
Hi Sweetie, everything's going fine up to now, experienced sooo much:) And we meet up soon, can't wait! Kisses from Kerman!

I have a stomachache and am feeling dizzy. Not from love but probably from the *kashk-e bademjan*, a delicious eggplant mush with yogurt that I ate for lunch in Bam. Was there something wrong with it? Accordingly, the soccer chat with three engineering students trying to convince me that Persepolis is awesome and Esteghlal is crap is decidedly lacking in passion, and within minutes I've forgotten their rationale. My host, Hussein, calls me and suggests that I take a cab to Azadi Square, and he will pick me up at the corner of Shariati Street.

At the busy junction, waiting for someone I know only from a credit card-sized photo on the Internet turns out to be a difficult task. Every other car halts and wants to give me a lift, all pro or opportunist cab drivers. (In Iran it's perfectly normal for people to earn a few rials, even without a license, by taking passengers, which is actually very practical, as no one in cities has to wait long for transportation.) Of course, they are all totally confused, as I don't give any clear hand signals but scrutinize them for similarities to the photo.

Twice I have to ask if the person behind the wheel happens to be called Hussein, and both times they speed off without a backward glance. I'm looking for someone who looks like a cross between a Bedouin and Jesus. The couchsurfing profile photo shows Hussein as a stern-faced, bearded man, with a heavy piece of cloth wrapped around his head and upper body. It is a highly aesthetic picture, worthy of National Geographic but not necessarily inviting. Apart from that, I know that he teaches graphic design at the university, is thirty years old, and dreams of traveling around the world taking pictures.

At long last a white Saipa stops, and the driver, with his jeans, shirt, and horn-rimmed glasses, although not Bedouin-like, does look very much like a designer. At least he's bearded.

89

"Stephan, hop in," says Hussein, while shoving some files and plastic bags to the side of the back seat. A young woman is sitting next to him. "We're on the way to a party. Is that okay with you?"

"Sure!" I reply.

He explains that he is going to see his friends for the first time in two weeks because they have all only recently returned from the end of *Nowruz* vacations with their families. Until he collected me he had been at the university, where this term he is lecturing on logos, the history of design, and poster design. I ask him for his thoughts on the Saipa logo on the steering wheel, which looks similar to the inside of a Mercedes star, with a few additional lines.

"It's really good, the concept of a famous Iranian designer. He discovered the symbol in a mosque in Shiraz," says Hussein. "Do you feel like going on a tour in the desert tomorrow? A friend of mine could arrange it."

We drive to Anis, one of Hussein's artist friends, who lives in a trendy, newly built neighborhood. The apartment consists of a large living room, with a kitchen niche, wooden blinds at every window, and a washroom. Large-format pictures of sad, twisted figures hang on the walls, and earrings and hairpins made of copper wire have been arranged on the kitchen table. There is so much handcrafted art that I have the impression of being at a private viewing and not an evening meal among friends.

"*Willkommen* in Kerman, *wie geht es dir?*" inquires a radiant Anis in fluent German, while pouring me a cup of chamomile tea. "I've been learning the language for eighteen months. I plan to join my husband in Austria soon and study art there."

I give Anis a pack of Lübeck marzipan, and she wants to know whether Lübeck is near Lüneberg.

"Yes, not so far away. Why?"

"I've got a few pictures hanging there." On her tablet she shows me some Facebook photos of her exhibition in Lüneberg that opened a few days prior. "I know an artist in Germany who arranged it." She would have liked to travel there for the opening but couldn't get a visa.

Despite the chamomile tea, my stomach is still feeling peculiar, and after being welcomed I have to make a dash for the washroom. On my return, Hussein opens a Persian-English translation program on his iPad and points enquiringly to the word "diarrhea." I nod unhappily. More and more guests arrive: Anis's husband, Reza; Mina and Taher; Moien, Hamed, and Nazanin, all designers and artists. The women wear wide pants and wide short-sleeved shirts, and they take off their veils as soon as they cross the threshold. Iranian women become prettier on entering a room; Iranian men become less handsome. The former because they take off their veils, the latter because they frequently swap their smart jeans for comfortable track pants or lurid Hawaiian shorts.

Anis makes me a tea with cinnamon, which is supposed to be good for the stomach. Then Hussein passes me a guitar—my online profile includes my love of guitar playing.

Apart from playing a few classical Spanish pieces, I don't contribute much to the entertainment this evening. I'm still suffering from outbreaks of sweat and stomach cramps. I have to rush to the washroom a second time no less quickly than the first time and spend four times as long there as usual. The same procedure on my return: Hussein with his translator program and serious face, and this time he has "Vomit, throw up" on the screen, and the picture of misery formerly known as Mr. Price nods resignedly. Mina rings her sister, a doctor. "She says if you have a temperature you will need an injection."

Taher feels my forehead and announces that there is no fever. All around me a feast of potato pancakes, yogurt, salads, and homemade cookies is served up; for me there is cinnamon tea, cola, and an apple of which I can only manage half.

Anis turns on the TV and selects the German ZDF news program. Jürgen Klopp is talking about the Champions League second leg soccer match, Dortmund against Real Madrid. "Sometimes we watch German TV to learn the language," says Anis. The weather forecast for the coming days is sixty to sixty-eight degrees Farenheit and then an ad for a laxative— very funny, TV channel ZDF.

Plates clatter, people laugh, and I am the only person comatose and most of the time unable to communicate. I feel like one of the sad, lonely, suffering figures in the paintings on the wall, with my head propped up against my hand. On top of everything, on clearing up I stumble over a glass on the floor, breaking it. What a troublesome guest I am. And Anis? As a parting gift she gives me one of her necklaces, with a blossom-shaped bronze ornament and a red wooden bead. "I hope you enjoy your time in Iran," she says.

THE DESERT

I **WAKE UP ON** a hard living room carpet, a neon light flickers lazily, my feet almost touching the gas oven on the wall. The room decoration is a battle between black-and-white photos, paintings, and objects that you might find in an anthropological museum. The alarm clock rings at seven, and Hussein makes a tea and hands over his keys.

"Get ready, Nasrin is coming to get you soon," he says.

Nasrin is a friend of his who, together with her two couchsurfing guests, is planning a trip to the desert. What I planned as a backpacking tour is becoming more and more an all-inclusive trip with pickup service and round-the-clock mentoring.

The doorbell rings, and I go down to a dusty parking bay surrounded by six-story apartment blocks. For the first time I see the dull facades in daylight. Nasrin is a spirited, tall and slightly rotund woman in her mid-thirties, wearing a black chador, white gloves, and blue sneakers.

Two Australians, Richard and Sally, who I figure are around fifty and thirty, respectively, welcome me from the back seat of

Nasrin's Peugeot. They have been traveling around the world for four years, having spent most of the time in Southeast Asia, very frequently couchsurfing. Nasrin's seven-year-old daughter, Kiana, is huddled between them. Nasrin teaches computer courses at the university and also works as an English teacher but has called in sick today so that she can show her guests the famous Dasht-e Loot desert. Such are the priorities of Iranians, the world champions of hospitality.

She speeds down the freeway between snow-capped mountains, with Michael Jackson and Beyoncé blaring from the radio. A driver, who hasn't realized that there is another highway ninety feet to our left for drivers going in his direction, speeds toward us. Nasrin gives a short lecture on men behind steering wheels. "They all think that they're the best drivers in the world. And when they see any female drivers they tailgate just to show them who's the boss."

On entering a tunnel, Nasrin tells us of a custom typical of the country: "In Iran we scream in tunnels." She starts shrieking, and three foreigners and a small girl join in. In a contest for the loudest scream, little Kiana is way ahead, so far ahead that I'm relieved not to be sitting next to her.

We leave the main road and meander through the mountainous landscape, passing through a couple of small villages. Soon the road straightens, and the route takes us through the increasingly barren steppes, which only seem a bit friendlier through the presence of isolated palm trees. We see dunes that are stabilized by highly resilient tamarisk plants, which can find enough nutrition in the sand to survive.

Nasrin knows the area like the back of her hand; she worked for a long time as a tourist guide, until her license was revoked because she was hosting couchsurfers. "It's illegal because the government is scared that we are hosting spies," she explains. Two years ago she took exactly the same route with guests from China, France, and Poland. After stopping at a salt river the car refused to start, and it was getting dark. "So I called the police, who said they couldn't send anybody. A couple truck drivers stopped every now and then, but nobody could help us." So she called the police again. "I started yelling at them: 'If I had said that there were a couple of young people drinking alcohol and dancing about you would have been here in minutes! But you won't lift a finger for a breakdown!' Then at least they gave me the number of a breakdown service, who eventually got us going."

Ultimately, however, the police were interested in what Nasrin was doing with the tourists. When it emerged that they were her guests, they withdrew her license as a tourist guide. "A friend of mine had it worse. He was a soldier and took guests to his military camp. He was caught and had to spend two months in prison."

Just after these remarks, Nasrin has to stop at a police station in Shahdad. "We have to register here," she says. "In case they ask who you are and how you know each other: you met, by chance, in Bam, and I'm your tourist guide," she directs.

The police, however, are less inquisitive than feared. As Nasrin shows them our passports, five heavily armed men in camouflage uniforms joke about what such an old man is doing traveling with such a young woman, that he is just trying to recapture his youth. Richard doesn't have a hair on his head, and you can certainly see that he has a twenty-year start on Sally. With all the excitement and banter about poor old Richard's adventure, they fail to notice that Nasrin's guide license hasn't been valid for two years. They ask her how much she is charging us but don't really believe her answer—nothing at all. However, they allow us to continue.

Adventurous Area appears on a traffic sign, and as if to underline this, shortly afterward another sign stating: *Nehbandan 170 miles*, the next town. "Actually, it's just three houses and a gas station," says Nasrin.

If you drive there, the only signs of civilization on the way will be the straight road, where you can see the oncoming traffic several minutes before crossing, and a power supply line. The tarmac shimmers in the heat, the ground appears to be covered by water, but on approach it just turns out to be a mirage. The perfectly straight desert road is like a metaphor for travel— when you reach a certain point that had seemed so alluring, then the next tempting stretch opens up just in front of you.

The sand formations all around become more and more bizarre—mountains towering ever higher at the roadside, the sand castles and rounded cupolas of the Dash-e Lut desert. "Reminds me a bit of the Outback," Richard remarks.

Another traffic sign announces: *Welcome to Gandom Beryan, the hottest area of the world.* The words *hottest area* and *world* have been erased, so presumably there is somewhere else that is even hotter.

On the couch. For two months—over and over again—I experience the hospitality of the Iranians.

A country beneath headscarves. In Iran quite a lot is different from the information that the news programs would have us believe.

The desert village of Kharanaq. Many places of interest have been spared mass tourism, until now.

"Are you on Facebook?" After two minutes of small talk, this young man passes me his tablet so that we can become online friends.

Fishing with Masoud, Darius, and Saler (right to left), on the vacation island of Kish.

A bit of a scoundrel. Has the actor Armin Mueller-Stahl been working recently as a cab driver in Kerman Province?

An overloaded passing maneuver. A day trip into the desert from Kerman.

Kaluts are impressive sandstone formations shaped over centuries by wind erosion.

The morning sun shining through colored glass at the Nasir-al Mulk mosque.

"Nowhere do I feel as free as in nature," says Saeed, a host from Shiraz.

A picnic at night. Many Iranians regularly break the laws and regulations—when they feel unobserved.

Always well grounded. During my travels I never slept on a couch and seldom in a bed.

An evening meal with couchsurfing hosts. The warmth of Iranians is unique.

Schoolkid in Abbas Abad. The everyday lives of people interest me far more than tourist attractions.

This also belongs to everyday life. You always have the feeling of being observed by two bearded men.

A *Scream* mask, Justin Bieber, and me. Time and again, it is fun looking at different apartments.

The ruins of Persepolis. About 2,500 years ago, Persia was the world's first superpower.

Yazd is particularly conservative. You see more women in chadors than in Tehran, Shiraz, or Isfahan.

The mausoleum of Sufi Shah Nimatullah Wali in Mahan. Even in spectacular places, I was often the only foreign tourist.

Photography and music. Girls in Shiraz and host Ahmad in Bushehr displaying their artistic skills.

Between a nuclear reactor and the sea. Bathers on the beach near the Bushehr power plant.

To the mosque? Always straight on. This sign shows believers the way.

At the battlefield center at Arvand Kenar, near the Iraq border, the soldiers never lose track of us.

Crownless date palms. The "trees of resistance" remain unfelled because of their symbolic power.

Bowing to the martyrs. The hundreds of thousands killed in the Iran-Iraq War are honored as heroes.

The Friday mosque in Yazd. "Don't even think about looking any women in the eyes." The warning of a colleague before I started my travels.

Unforgettable encounters. Little Azadeh in Kermanshah and Sophie in Isfahan.

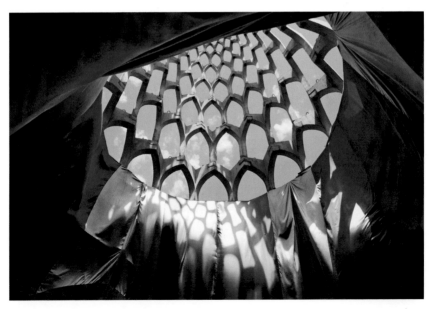

A view of the sky from the "Tomb of the Eight Unknown Soldiers," from the battle of Fath ol-Mobin.

A Kurdish smuggler on the border with Iraq. A few hours later, I am very relieved to have taken so many horse pictures.

There is always time for tea in Iran. For instance, in the idyllic village of Hajij.

Not only is the site of the village spectacular but also the colorful clothes of the locals.

Probably soon tourists will be bused in, but for the time being, it is still very traditional.

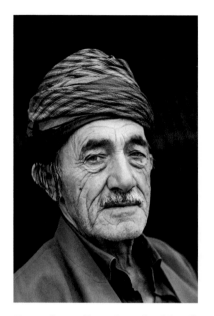

Faces that tell stories. The friendliness of the Iranians leaves a deep impression.

Sheep at the roadside. The herd will travel more than six hundred miles to the north.

Modern Iran. Fast food is extremely popular with the younger generation. In every large city there are countless burger joints and Kentucky Fried Chicken copies.

Date in a living room. Mona from Hamedan (left), with extended family.

"Let's have some fun!" Host Funman lives up to his nickname (left, with wife, Mahboube).

My sleeping area was in a rundown house in the middle of an overgrown garden.

Tehran, the metropolis with 10 million inhabitants, is the beginning and the end of my travels.

Evening impressions on the Caspian Sea. Women bathe here fully veiled.

Darkness and light. Iran enchants and infuriates simultaneously, and it rewards every visitor with unforgettable experiences.

"Over 158 degrees Fahrenheit has been measured here. We say that you can fry an egg on the ground," says Nasrin.

We soon reach the Shur salt river, the site of the bad memories of the breakdown two years ago. It is some fifteen feet wide and at no point deeper than a few inches. Salt forms in clumps, looking like slushy snow on the banks. A little farther away, in the sand crusty white plates have formed, and tourists have left footprints or messages in Persian, and a truck driver has left a huge tire. The thermometer in the car registers nearly 98 degrees Fahrenheit. Luckily, it's windy today.

On the trip back, we stop at a particularly spectacular sand mountain, with vertical walls that seem to have grown out of the ground and not been formed by centuries of wind and erosion. We can only see a fraction of the natural sand mountains; they stretch ninety miles from north to south. The biggest ones are as high as ten-story buildings. On the horizon of this desert wonderland you can see a snow-capped peak. Below, one of the two or three hottest areas of the world; above, ice cold—an "Adventure Area" that is pretty rich in contrasts.

While taking a stroll in the sand, Richard remarks that one of the disadvantages of couchsurfing is that you never have time for yourself and always have to arrange yourself around the plans of others, which is why they sometimes stay in hotels. "But the advantages far outweigh the disadvantages," says Sally. She recommends a host in Chabahar, in southeast Iran, if I am ever in the area. He has very few guests, which was why he looked after them so impressively. He even took the Australians to a traditional Baluchestan wedding. "Colorful robes, complete segregation of the sexes, and an exuberant rifle salute," says Richard.

97

Back in Shadad we buy some ice cream and Istak apple malt beer, and Nasrin adds some delicious *kolompeh* (date cookies) that her sister baked. Then back to the police station to deregister. The second contact with the authorities is also very different from expectations. First, they rummage through the trunk of Nasrin's Peugeot. "They are looking for alcohol and opium," our nonlicensed guide explains.

But maybe they just wanted to check how much space was free. A policeman asks whether it would be a nuisance to take a few things to the next police station in Sirch. A short while later, five heavily armed young men load up the car with canned vegetables and large cartons of chicken meat. We deliver the goods ten miles down the road to a young policeman whose sluggish movements imply that we have disturbed his siesta. Or is he simply a typical Kermani? "People here are considered to be especially lazy. We blame the lack of oxygen; the city is 5,500 feet above sea level," says Nasrin. But there could be another explanation: in Iran they joke that so much opium is smoked in Kerman that airline passengers get high just flying above the city.

Nasrin has two more highlights for us—a hill with a sign stating that *one of the Supreme Leaders of the whole Islamic World, Ayatollah Khomeini, walked up here and sat on a boulder. Allah, bless the stone.* And a store that sells vanilla ice cream with carrot juice, which tastes much better than it sounds.

Back at Hussein's home I treat myself to an afternoon nap. Afternoon naps are something very Iranian. Normally, I never sleep at this time, and the fact that I'm so tired must have something to do with the low-oxygen air of Kerman.

From: Hussein Kermanv
Hello Stephan, I'll come home late, a friend had an accident

Hussein gets home at 10:30 PM. He has bought mushrooms and ground meat, and makes a sandwich filling. "I'm so sorry everything took such a long time," he says. "A friend was run over by a cab in Azadi Square and broke his leg. He had to have an operation, but he's doing all right now. Would you like a beer?"

Hussein gets a pint bottle of Delster malt beer. He opens it, and there is a loud hiss of escaping gas. His homemade brew is frothy and pretty sweet, but it's not too bad. "I add yeast and 3.5 ounces of sugar per bottle. I leave it for three days next to the gas oven and then decant it into bottles. Every now and then I let the gas out of the bottles, and after a couple more days I have my beer," explains the man whose profile photo looks like Jesus and who can turn fizzy drinks to beer. "But I have to be careful; if I'm caught, I get eighty lashes."

BUREAUCRACY

THE NEXT DAY, on my way to the Management of Foreigners Affairs Office, I ask myself how many lashes I would get
for deception on a visa application. If I don't want to fly back
soon, I have to extend my visitor's permit. In the consulate in
Germany they only gave me twenty days. A line has formed in
front of the green steel door leading to the office, but one of
the employees beckons me to follow him. I have to leave my
cell phone and camera at reception and receive a brass token
with a three-figure number and a picture of a cell phone on it.
A soldier leads me via an inner courtyard to an office, where
there are a few mounted seats and a wobbly metal fan as a
cooling system. Behind a wooden desk, two employees, a man
and a woman, receive visa applications and passports.

The visa form requires my profession and my address in
Iran. I fill in "website editor" and "Omid Guesthouse, Esteghlal Lane, Kerman." If I had written *journalist*, I could forget
about a visa extension, and a private address would have
raised suspicions. I feel like I'm taking an exam at school, with

the difference that instead of getting bad marks, I would have to leave the country earlier than planned, or even risk getting into trouble with the Iranian justice system, which is well known for not being squeamish in the handling of offenders. Under "reasons for travel" I fill in "tourism." My guidebook says that one applicant had foolishly written "to visit my Iranian girlfriend"—his visa was declined on moral grounds.

"You have to deposit thirty thousand toman at the Melli Bank and return with the receipt and two passport photos," says the official. "The bank is just around the corner, Edalat Street." He waves vaguely left and gives me a handwritten note with the account number 217 115 395 5007.

How to ask for directions

- Look for pedestrians between twenty-five and forty-five (the younger they are, the greater the probability that they speak English).
- In case no English speakers are available, repeat the sentence: *"Salam, Melli Bank kodja ast?"* Instead of Melli Bank, you can insert any preferred place or street name.
- The passerby will gesticulate in a particular direction. You can be fairly sure that plus or minus ninety degrees the direction is right.
- After five hundred feet ask someone else; he will probably put you on a slightly different course (possibly a better approximation).
- Always remember that Iranians prefer to give a wrong answer to no answer.
- By the third to fifth helper you should have a fairly good indication of where to go. By the way, cab drivers use

101

exactly the same strategy—they never trust the first source of information.

· · · · · · · · · ·

AT THE BANK I have to collect a number tag and wait for an LED light display to show my number. I give the clerk the note with the handwritten account number, give him thirty thousand toman, and then he passes me the receipt. On the way back I go to the photo store. The examples hanging on the wall, portraits of people resting their chins on the clenched fist of their left hand, leave no doubt about the photographer's specialty. They all look a little like mediocre crooners. Luckily, I'm allowed to keep my arms down. I return to the visa building with my photos and receipt, hand in my camera and cell phone and then the necessary papers and my passport. "Come back at twelve," says the official. It's only just ten.

102   "Come back at two," she says at twelve. "My boss is at a meeting, and he needs to sign the document." This means more time to find out that I'm a journalist by a simple process of googling. The guidebook says that the visa offices

sometimes use Google. As a distraction, I wander through the bazaar. Describing a Middle Eastern bazaar in every detail is like carrying cumin to Kerman—there are an incredible number of stores, goods, aromas, and sellers. And in this case a charming teahouse based on the old Hamam teahouses. The smell of hookah smoke, a fountain, ornate columns, and a man playing a santur, a kind of hammered Persian dulcimer. As I enter, he glances at me and begins to play a melody from *The Godfather*—I assume because it has a European feel to it and not because he is implying that there is something criminal about me.

Shortly before two: a renewed trip to the visa offices, hand in cell phone and camera, get my brass token, all routine now. After a few minutes "Mr. Estefan" is announced, and I get back my passport, with a new stamp: *The visa is extended up to 17.5.2014.* I'm as happy as if I'd just won a four-week dream vacation, which in some way is true. But of course you wouldn't know it—exuberance and dancing about would be considered improper in the Management of Foreigners Affairs Office.

From: Iran
lammina,frendmobina.came hear inHerat. Emamstreet

From: Laila Hamburg
Hey honey, my flight lands at 21:00 in Yazd. See you tomorrow night!

I spend the afternoon on a tour of the small town of Mahan, rightly famous for a Sufi dervish named Shah Nimatullah Wali and wrongly for the Bagh-e Shahzadeh Gardens. Iranians are always turned on by the color green, which is why the garden compound, with a couple cherry trees, wilting flowers, and a mud-colored cascade, is such a popular attraction. Actually, the only spectacular thing about it is its location at the foot of some mountains. The cab driver bringing me back to Kerman has far more character, with his white mustache, suit, and hat. He drives his ancient Paykan and feeds me sweet, gooey clumps of halvah while the sun sinks behind the mountain peaks to the west. Of course, he cheats me at the end of the ride, but the price is worth it just for the souvenir photo.

FAKE MARRIAGE

THE BUS ONLY needed a spritely 5.5 hours for the 250 miles to Yazd. On arrival I book a double room at the Orient Hotel and buy a plastic rose with I *love you* on its plastic leaves at a souvenir store. The streets of the desert city are alive with a hectic hustle-bustle of activity. Fruit stalls, fast-food joints, carpet dealers. Two groups of European tourists, one Italian and one Swiss, pass by, an unusual sight after weeks with the locals. They seem very foreign and a bit ungainly, especially the women. You can see from a distance that they haven't really become accustomed to their Islamic garments.

To: Laila Hamburg
Hey baby, tell the cabdriver to take you to the Orient Hotel, next to masjed-e jameh. See you soon!:*

The room isn't exactly a honeymoon suite—separate beds, bare interior, and a mosque picture on the wall. The only cause for slightly romantic thoughts is the fact that the washroom door cannot be closed and sometimes opens on a whim. To compensate for this, the inner courtyard is amazing: a burbling fountain, caravanserai-like arcades, and an undisturbed view of the star-studded heavens.

I got to know Laila, who is half Iranian, more than a year ago in Hamburg through couchsurfing. I was looking for couchsurfers from my city who had some connection to Iran so that I could learn more about the country. In her profile she described herself as "spontaneous and dreamy," and as someone who couldn't live without music. We met a few times and discovered that she was coincidentally going to be in Iran at the same time as me. During a boozy evening in February we decided to spend a week traveling together. And to get married. Well, not exactly. The arrangement that she captured with a pen on a coaster was for a ten-day fake marriage and purely for a number of practical reasons: tourists to Iran can only book a double room in a hotel as husband and wife; it would save a lot of explanations in conversations with the locals; and last but not least, because it would save Laila from a host of unwelcome advances. She had already traveled to Iran a couple times and knew the feeling of being fair game when making excursions without an escort. An amusing side effect of our "engagement" is that since then we have called each other "honey" and "sweetie," and we make a genuine effort to cultivate quirks that you can only find with real couples.

Instead of arriving by cab, she comes in a private car. A fellow passenger on the flight offered to give her a lift to the hotel. "Leave you alone for a few days and look what happens," I say as we shake hands in front of the hotel. I ask, despite her new acquaintance, whether she still is prepared to marry me. "Yes, why not," is her answer. Then it's enough of the formal nonsense: "Great to see you!" And we hug each other, in the middle of the street, in the middle of Iran; at this moment, we couldn't care less.

Laila is twenty-nine, wearing a red scarf over a loose-fitting pink garment, and she works as a graphic designer. Her father comes from Tehran, and her mother is German. She has spent her whole life in Hamburg but speaks a little Persian.

We carry her luggage to the room. If she is pleased about the plastic rose, she doesn't show it, promptly dumping the present unceremoniously in the trash can. We then go for a walk through a labyrinth of sand-colored alleyways while we exchange travel adventures. I tell of fishing on Kish, dominatrices, and smuggler buses, and she of her overprotective family in Tehran and strenuous hosts. "In Chalus, in north Iran, there was one host who took me on a tour in the mountains. He desperately wanted me to take off my veil. Well, okay— no problem. He took some photos. When the path became tricky he took my hand. But when he wanted to kiss me, things began to get really unpleasant. Not that I was frightened of him—he was totally insecure, and I think that he simply wanted to touch a woman once in his life."

Behind a half-open wooden door some steps lead up to a flat roof with a cupola. A few Iranians are already there: two young men and two young women, smoking slim cigarettes and holding hands. Not wanting to disturb them, we sit on the other side of the igloo-sized cupola.

There are moments during traveling when the allure of wanderlust wanes but waits for you, suddenly popping up exactly where you are. Where future and past no longer matter, and you believe that your path, up to this point, has been a circuitous and zigzagging journey to reach this particular place, and all that follows is nothing more than a lengthy departure. When you already suffer from yearning while still there.

I am not usually the type who sits around gazing at the scenery. Almost all of my top ten unforgettable travel experiences are in some way connected to activities.

But in Yazd I learn something: sitting on a flat roof and gazing at the scenery is the most beautiful thing in the world. We should all spend more time sitting on roofs and gazing.

In best-case scenarios we would be looking out over a place like Yazd. A mud brick–colored city with magnificent minarets and mosque cupolas lit up with purple light, with no skyscrapers obscuring the view and a mountain range presiding on the horizon. Yazd is so beautiful that even the air conditioners are grand buildings—the *badgirs*, wind catchers, looking like gigantic ancient microphones create natural ventilation through slits at the tops of the towers. Every now and then the call to prayers of the muezzins, who really can sing, pierce the quiet of the evening desert air. You just have to climb a few stairs and you feel free, far away from all of the restrictions and laws. But this freedom is deceptive; Yazd is a very religious and conservative city. And hostile to couchsurfing. A couple months ago the manager of the Silk Road Hotel complained to the police that private accommodation was killing off his business. Since then the authorities have been harsher on members than elsewhere; there have been interrogations and arrests. I wrote quite a few e-mails, but it was impossible to find a host in Yazd. One wrote back that unfortunately he couldn't help me out as he was too scared.

And so Laila and I are sitting in this magical place, talking about fear. "My aunt and uncle in Tehran are always incredibly worried about me and would rather not let me out without company," she says. "And I notice that this fear is rubbing off on me. When a country is ruled by such strict regulations, then in time it takes over your thoughts. I'm always thinking about whether something I'm doing could be wrong or dangerous." Yesterday she noticed that her German website was blocked in Iran. Type in the address, then an error message appears in Persian, and then a few nature photos fade in. "I'm wondering whether the secret service is collecting information about me. Or whether it's because I posted a few pictures of scantily dressed women." Fear and paranoia are the strongest weapons of totalitarian regimes, and the *mullahs* are real pros at using them.

I watch a couple of women in chadors fifty feet below us as they walk through an arch illuminated in green and ask myself if they, too, are afraid in their everyday lives. Whether they belong to those who believe in the system in which they live or to those who secretly dream of freedom. Our rooftop perspective feels like being in balcony seats at the theater. Showing tonight: the ten thousandth repeat of the play *Islamic Republic*, showing every day throughout the country, with a cast of millions, all well-trained performers. A masquerade without dance, a tragedy without applause, a plot without conclusion. And no one knows what is going on in the heads behind the masks.

· · · · · · · · · ·

THE NEXT DAY we buy wedding rings at a street stall for one dollar. On the opposite side of the street a popcorn vendor waits for customers.

"Did you know that the Persian word for popcorn is "elephant farts"? asks Laila.

No, I didn't. I notice that the men in Yazd always greet and address me first. Laila mainly appears to be seen as an ornamental accessory. However, as she is the one who speaks Persian, she often takes over the conversation after a few sentences. Someone selling kebabs is so enchanted by her that he promptly conjures up a cousin (with lots of gel in his hair and the top button of his shirt open), who drives us to our next destination, the Dowlat Abad Garden. His car is a black Mazda sports car with black leather seat covers. In one of the side pockets there is a bottle of cologne. The passenger seat is more like a passenger lounger, and the center console a light-blinking monster with a navigational aid the size of an iPad.

"Phew! I wouldn't have got in without you," Laila says.

"Without your Persian, I wouldn't be here, either," I reply.

"We're a super team," she says and laughs.

"I think our driver fancies you; he was ogling you in the rear-view mirror."

It's Murphy's Law of love that from the moment people start a relationship, they automatically become one or two degrees more attractive to the opposite sex. Shortly after saying goodbye to "Mazda Man" a group of conscripts in camouflage uniforms hanging around at a ticket window wave Laila over. They ask if they can take a photo with us. According to Laila, the most handsome guy is named Bijan and is twenty.

"Sports car drivers, men in uniform—aren't there any clichés that are below you?" I ask.

"Yes, authors," she says. And we haven't even been married twenty-four hours.

Five minutes later she is no longer laughing, as a black-veiled young woman walking arm in arm with a female friend greets me with: "You're beautiful, handsome!" and offers me *gaz*, a sugary confection with pistachios, a specialty of Isfahan. She is named Elaheh, is quite pretty, and tells me that she is studying medical sciences in Isfahan before grinning and sashaying back to her companion.

Now it's Laila's turn to look at me critically. With an innocent look I try to give the impression that I didn't do anything, and that I have no idea what's just happened.

We walk through the 250-year-old gardens of the then governor, past cypress trees, pomegranate shrubs, and an artificial watercourse that splits the compound in two. It is dominated by a hexagonal reception palace with pretty pavilions, colored glass windows, and the tallest badgir wind catcher in Iran, 110 feet high. A couple horizontal timber struts have been added for stability, which the pigeons are thankful to use as perches.

From: Iran
hi,whereisyounow? Pleasecome, harat.iamfrendsmobina.
iseeyourpicture

"Laila, there's something else."
"Yes, what's up, then?"
"I've got two admirers, and I need your help."
"Interesting."
"Can you translate a few questions?"
"You're crazy."

To: Iran
Salam mina, khubi? Chand sall dari? Shoghlat chie? Tu
waghte azad che kar mikoni?

There is little left to mention of Yazd, except that large
amounts of the cold dessert *faloodeh*, made from thin noo-
dles and a semifrozen syrupy mixture of sugar and rose water,
cause stomachaches, that there are unique circular raised structures on which the Zoroastrians used to burn corpses, and that
camel goulash tastes exactly the same as any other goulash.

In the course of our fake marriage, we have quickly
developed routines and behavioral patterns that take other
newlyweds years to hone.

Breakfast. I yell from one buffet table to another: "Where
shall we sit, honey? Our usual place?"

It is a bad mistake in a foreign country to feel too secure
about not being understood. I get an irritated, quizzical look
from a tourist sitting at a nearby table before she quickly turns
her head away. On passing her table I glance down and notice
that she has just written ALEMANIA on the bottom right-hand
side of a postcard, so for sure she knows my language.

112

After so many nights in private apartments I can't really enjoy staying in a hotel, even if the bed is much more comfortable than any carpet. The friendliness of the staff feels different from the friendliness of my hosts because I pay them to be nice to me. They are the sellers, and I am the buyer, hoping for good value for my money. If the quality is not right, then I get annoyed. If the price is right, I'm happy. I have different expectations from a one-hundred-dollar room than from a twenty-dollar room. The psychology of a couchsurfing visit is very different, as I can only win. I don't pay anything, so I expect no more than a six-square-foot sleeping space. Up to now I have had much more than that every time.

From: Iran

salamshafa.khubam.shomakhube.madaram14sal.shn-machandsal dare? manmeravam madrese

I ask Laila to translate. She looks at my cell phone and starts laughing. It takes a while until she gets her breath back: "Hello, Shafa. I'm well. How are you? I'm fourteen. How old are you? I'm still at school."

"Oh, maybe the love of my life isn't waiting for me in Harat, after all."

"Yes, I agree," says Laila.

LOST IN TRANSPORTATION III

SOMEWHERE BETWEEN YAZD and Shiraz we decide to hitch-hike for a couple hundred miles. A spectacular failure. Not because no one wants to give us a lift. The first car that we wave down stops (we waved because the usual raised thumb ritual is considered an offensive gesture, at least by the older generations, so the chances of a lift are low).

The driver introduces himself as Gorlam and indicates that we should hop in. "I live just around the corner. Would you like some tea?" he asks. After half a mile he stops in front of a whitewashed house with a flat roof.

In the living room Gorlam's four-year-old son, Iman, is doing a couple circuits on his kiddie bike. The wall is deco-rated with sayings from the *Quran* and photos of well-dressed sons with well-dressed wives. To one side of the room there is a kind of bathtub full of potted plants. When Iman pauses from his circuits he proves to be incredibly talkative but unfortunately fails to understand that I haven't got a clue what he's saying. Fatimeh, his mother, brings a plate of huge slices of melon. Gorlam says that he has to go quickly to his office; he works for the highways department. We talk to Fatimeh, or rather Laila does, and I just sit around. People who can only say car, fish, and elephant farts in Persian automatically become outsiders and observers in such situations.

Laila explains where we come from, how beautiful it was in Yazd, and that we are now heading for Shiraz. "We've known each other for two years and have been married one year," she fibs.

It is more difficult to explain what hitchhiking is all about, although we had looked up the word *ootostop* beforehand. The concept doesn't seem to be known here. Fatimeh, anyway, doesn't react to it. "You have to take a cab to Safa Shahr and then take a bus to Shiraz," she explains. "You can spend the night here and then take the bus tomorrow morning. It's not so tiring."

It is only just 1 PM, and we would really like to be on the move. Staggering hospitality is not compatible with the wish of traveling more than half a mile today. But Fatimeh remains indefatigable. She offers to call her sister, who works in a hotel in Shiraz and can organize accommodation for us. Laila says that we already have a room. If we had begun to explain our idea of sleeping at the homes of locals we only met on the Internet, our benefactor would have thought us completely mad.

Fatimeh serves up tea and goodies, and she asks whether we would change our minds and stay for something to eat. We politely decline but decide to wait for Gorlam's return before traveling on.

All in all we spend 2.5 hours with the nice family. At the end we film a video message with a cell phone and are asked a further six times to share a meal with them. As we turn them down for the sixth time, Fatimeh and Gorlam are visibly disappointed. They ask again if we are really sure we can manage without a hotel in Shiraz and whether it might not be better to stay overnight with them.

Back on the road it doesn't take a minute before the next lift is offered. This time the car turns out to be a cab, but there is already one passenger, and we can travel the three or four miles to the next village for nothing. Our fellow passenger, Mohsen, a math teacher, gets out of the cab with us. He also wants to go a short way toward Shiraz and suggests that we share a taxi, as there is no other possibility of making headway. He also reacts with a puzzled shaking of the head to the term ootostop. We agree to share, and so after 2.5 miles in three hours, our Iranian hitchhiking adventure draws to a close. It would have been quicker to walk.

HIDE-AND-SEEK

"**BE QUIET AND** don't speak English on the street; otherwise, the neighbors will hear you," says Saeed. "It's forbidden to take in foreigners." He jumps out of the car, looking left and right like a burglar, and unlocks the steel door to his apartment in southwest Shiraz. Then he waves to us to quickly come in. We snatch our backpacks and scurry to the entrance. Saeed's friend, who picked us up in the city center in his car, says goodbye and disappears into the night.

Saeed is twenty, a graphic design student, and "pretty hot," as Laila put it on seeing his profile photo—black wispy hair, bushy eyebrows, knockout smile. After reading one of my posts in a couchsurfing forum, he contacted me to ask me whether I wanted to stay with him during my trip to Shiraz.

According to what I read of his profile, Saeed likes kickboxing, BMX bikes, and juggling, and apart from that he is an absolute couchsurfing junkie. In the last three months he has had forty-five guests, has organized meetings, and is always traveling around his country with a tent and a backpack.

Saeed has another guest. Christian, lounging on the carpet, is in his mid-twenties. He has a designer beard, is from Colombia, and manages to simultaneously look incredibly tired and incredibly happy. Travel drunk and high from the road. He quit his job as a business consultant four months ago and now jets around the world. Kenya, Tanzania, Ethiopia, Djibouti, Egypt, Turkey. Iran was the only country on his route that his mother told him to contact her every two days to say that he was still alive.

"There is a parallel: Colombia also has a bad reputation, and everyone immediately thinks of cocaine, drug barons, and criminals. But the country has so much to offer. High mountains, dream beaches, fantastic nature, and lively cities. But a lot of people are scared to go there," says Christian.

"I've had some guests here who have kept their destination secret from their parents," says Saeed. "People think there's a terrorist hiding in every corner, and that our favorite leisure activity is burning American and Israeli flags. It's nonsense." He makes some black tea in his samovar. A narrow kitchenette

118

separates the two rooms of the tubular apartment. On the shelf there are mussel shells from the Persian Gulf, a Rubik's Cube, juggling balls, and a considerable collection of foreign coins: cents, lira, rupees, pesos. The front door has been screened with aluminum foil, the apartment has one window to the back that has been masked by cardboard, and a door to the inner courtyard is hidden behind a dark red drape.

"The police here are pretty unpleasant, though" says Christian. "I was sitting on a bench with an Iranian friend in Tehran when two officials came up to us and took some photos. They didn't say a word; they probably just wanted to intimidate us."

"Every day I expect to find the police at my door because of all my guests," says Saeed. "I'm prepared for it. But until then I will have as many guests as I want—five to ten a month."

He is not afraid when traveling inside Iran, even in the danger zones in the borderlands to Pakistan and Afghanistan. "Actually, I would like to be kidnapped; it would certainly be interesting," he says.

"I wouldn't agree with that about Colombia," Christian maintains.

"I suppose that in Iran even the kidnappers are pretty tolerable hosts," I suggest.

"You would probably have better chances than me to find that out," adds Saeed. Do I sense a bit of envy in his voice? "Iranians are not so interesting. These criminals know that our government won't cough up. Europeans are much more lucrative."

Shiraz is one of the few cities in the world that you can recognize blindfolded because it smells of oranges. Not only in the gardens and parks, but even on roads with heavy traffic; it seems as if someone has tried to neutralize the exhaust fumes with a citrus spray. Even Iran's national poet, Hafiz, found the place pleasant to the nose:

> Shiraz, and the stream of Ruknabad,
> and that fragrant breeze—Disparage it not,
> for it is the beauty-spot of the seven regions![1]

It smells of oranges, for example, near the fortress in the center, which was built in the eighteenth century during the reign of Karim Khan Zand. He made Shiraz his capital and went down in history as a comparatively peace-loving, just, and even modest Persian king.

Laila and I are waiting for Hamed on some grass between beds of flowers in front of a leaning round tower and some massive fortress walls.

This morning at ten o'clock I posted a message on the Shiraz couchsurfing forum: *Hello, we are 2 incredibly nice Germans, and we would be incredibly happy to wander through the city today with someone local.* I added my cell phone number, which wasn't particularly clever, at least in view of the resulting problems of organizing the meetings offered.

From: Unknown Number
hi.i would be happy to hang out with u, any time you say.
Negar cs Shiraz

From: Unknown Number
Hey Stephan. This is Soroush from Shiraz. I've just came back from a 6 months hitchhiking trip around Iran and Iraq. I'll be more than happy to meet you and hear about your stories. I impressed by your profile by the way.

From: Unknown Number
hey stephan, i can meet u around 6 pm. Reza

From: Unknown Number
Hello Stephan & Laila Hope u enjoyd Shiraz so far This is
Amin frm cs. would be nice if u join me & my guests to get
to go fr something fun this aftrnoon:-)

What is the opposite of shitstorm? Lovestorm? Four text
messages in only two hours. Slowly, I get the feeling that a sec-
retary might be useful for organizing our schedule. On top of
the messages there were two phone calls. One of them I didn't
understand a single word, and I wasn't even sure which language the man at the other end of the line was speaking. And
one from Hamed, with whom we arranged to meet at noon in
front of the fortress. Once again there is the usual blind date
problem. We haven't the faintest idea what our new friend
looks like or even how old he is, but we are continuously
approached. "Welcome to Iran. Where do you come from? Are
you enjoying your trip?"

But also: "I'm a registered tourist guide. Ooooh, Germany!
I have friends in Frankfurt and Berlin. What would you like to
see?" Friendliness with ulterior motives. In many other destinations it is so commonplace that you automatically quicken
your pace as soon as you hear, "Hey, Mister." I wonder whether
tourist money will one day corrupt the natural Iranian warmth,
leading to the melodramatic "my friend" affectation of a sunglasses vendor on a sandy beach. Every year more visitors
arrive with more wallets, exchanging money for the magic of
the country, and all of them will take a bit of this magic home,
so that in the end less and less magic will remain.

Recently, this has happened in Myanmar as tourism sky-rocketed, thanks to political stability. Now, possibly, it is Iran's turn, also because countries like Syria, Libya, or Iraq, countries that were similarly attractive to people interested in the Middle East, are no longer options because of terror and war. Since 2013 the number of people visiting Iran has reached new records every year, and today there are not enough hotel beds for the tourists.

Hamed has no trouble recognizing us. The only other foreigners in front of the fortress is a group of Taiwanese tourists. Hamed is thirty-one, with brown leather shoes and an expensive shirt. The tourist in me is overjoyed about his enormous expertise on buildings and plant life in Shiraz. The husband in me registers the brown bedroom eyes and the hand that time and again casually brushes against Laila's back while the son of a bitch explains the significance of symmetrical structures in Persian architecture or makes remarks like: "Sadly, at the bazaar nowadays there's far too much 'Made in China.' You have to know where to find the good stuff."

So he shows us a stall selling ornately carved backgammon boards, and then two gardens are on the program. In the first one, on the grounds of Qavam House, it smells even more orangey than in the rest of the city. One look in the mirrored porch reminds me of the necessity of shaving. The skin on Hamed's face by comparison could be used in a Gillette ad. I console myself with the beautiful women on the upper level, the ones painted on the wall and framed by ornamental flowers. They wear robes, their shoulders bare, and have luxurious locks of hair and white lower arms. No Islamic dress, no headscarves—I catch myself, for a fraction of a second, feeling slightly outraged.

POETRY

FROM THE ORANGE garden we take a cab to Bagh-e Eram. *Eram* translates to heaven or paradise, but Cypress Gardens would be just as fitting. Tuscany would be proud of such specimens. The paved paths between artificial ponds and streams serve as catwalks for youngsters, with their Justin Bieber hairstyles and perfectly groomed beards (the boys) or their expensive scarves, perched way back on their heads, and bare ankles (the girls). And tons of makeup. "What shall I bring her? A beautiful face needs nor jewels nor mole nor the tiring-maid's art,"[1] wrote Hafiz, the most famous of all Shirazis, in the fourteenth century. The statement is still valid today.

Flute music lilts from loudspeakers, nightingales sing in the trees, and date palms sway in the evening breeze. Sometimes Iran lays it on a bit thick, and so it is in this "Paradise Park." At the entrance there is a man with two budgie-sized yellow birds who pick out colored cards with Hafiz sayings from a small plastic tub. It is a much-loved way of reading your horoscope. There is a wonderful tradition in Iran whereby many people use Hafiz tomes rather like fortune cookies; they randomly open the book and select a saying. I give the man twenty thousand rial, and the beak of destiny selects a purple note. Hamed translates:

Ask to what goal the wandering dervish hies,
They knew not his desire who counselled thee: Question his rags no more![2]

Beneath it there is an explanation of the verse: *It is better to stick to your path than always trying something new and deviating from the right way. Only those who adhere to the words of the wise one will succeed.* For me and my travels I manage to put a different slant on his wisdom: *As I'm not a clever dervish and don't know the way, I will continue to deviate from the path and knock at any Iranian door that pleases me.* He's a good man, that Hafiz.

The mausoleum of the poet is in a walled compound in the north of the city. Hafiz, whom Goethe considered his twin brother, rests in a pavilion with eight pillars beneath a white marble slab. Today there are many elementary school classes here. Kids in lovely school uniforms lay their hands on the gravestone and recite verses. Laila and I are not the only newlyweds. Hafiz is a kind of patron of lovers, which is why many Iranians make a pilgrimage to Shiraz shortly after marrying. Our conversation is presumably untypical of the usual whisperings of couples.

The dress regulations are getting on Laila's nerves. "I've been wearing the same stuff for five days now, always this red scarf and this dumb, wide frumpy robe."

"Before we were married you made more of an effort with your outfits."

"You, too! Need I mention gray hiking pants—every day!"

"Do you love me anyway?"

"No."

A women is holding a small book and reading out quatrains. The language is like music, and even if you don't understand the words, it doesn't detract from the flowing beauty of the sound. Admiration of Hafiz unifies religious and less devout people; they simply interpret his words differently. When Hafiz enthuses about wine and drunkenness, for one it is a metaphor for the intoxicating experience of God, and for the other a homage to forbidden pleasures. The poet was a prominent scholar of the *Quran* and a man of the world at the same time, so probably both interpretations are not totally wrong. At schools, however, there's not much Hafiz on the curriculum. "There's a lot about alcohol and changing the world for his own pleasures," says Hamed.

I have a translation of some of his works with me and leaf through it.

The ancient world shall turn to youth again,
And other wines from out Spring's chalice flow;
Wine-red, the judas-tree shall set before

The pure white jessamine a brimming cup,
And wind flowers lift their scarlet chalice up
For the star-pale narcissus to adore."[3]

I find a few lines that I have to read out to Laila:

Arise, oh Cup-bearer, rise!
And bring to the lips that are thirsting the bowl they praise,
For it seemed that love was an easy thing,
But my feet have fallen on difficult ways.[4]

Laila laughs.

How to make small talk for beginners

Irani: Hello, mister!
Answer: *Salam!* (Smile.)
Irani: Unintelligible sentence containing the word *Farsi*.
Answer: *Man farsi balad nistam.* (Apologetically hunch shoulders, palms pointing up.)
Irani: Unintelligible sentence not containing the word *Farsi*.
Answer: *Aleman!* (Point at yourself.)
Irani: *Aleman!* Germany! Very Good! Welcome to Iran!
Answer: Merci! (Smile.)

· · · · · · · · ·

126 **IT WOULD BE** beyond my scope to give a detailed account of all the talks and encounters in the city of poetry, yet so many of these keyhole insights into the lives of young Iranians are worth mentioning.

There is the literature student, Golbarg, who wants to write her thesis on gender issues and feminism but doubts whether her themes will be accepted. "There are lecturers who support me, but as soon as there is any attempt even to mention homosexuality, you can forget it. Absolutely impossible in Iran," she says.

Or Soroush, a good friend of Saeed, a traveler seeking adventure, who contacted me per text messages. He has just returned from a hitchhiking trip to Karbala in Iraq, the holiest city for Shia Muslims. "Everyone there has fifteen mattresses. I was invited to stay everywhere, a new host every night," he says. He doesn't seem to be too bothered by what others consider dangerous destinations. His next trip will take him close to the Pakistani border. "I would rather live every day to the fullest than a hundred years of boredom," he continues. And then, almost in passing, he pinpoints the central problem of my own travels, but also maybe something that makes it interesting. "The best thing about hitchhiking is that you really learn about the people of a particular country. The rich and poor, conservative and modern. With couchsurfing, on the other hand, you are only dealing with one group, who is educated and speaks English, is very modern and enthusiastic about the Internet."

There is Negar, who also texted me. She is a biologist, likes Jane Austen, and plays the piano, but she would rather be a singer. But nothing will come of that, as her father, afraid of whispering in the family, has forbidden her from performing with her choir. In Iran women are not allowed to sing solo in public, and even in a group it is frowned upon by conservatives. She complains that in Iran education is encouraged but not excellence. Those who are clever often have worse chances

in top positions and are intentionally marginalized. "By making it clear that it's not worth standing out, the government
fosters a climate of lethargy, and lethargy is well suited to the
maintenance of power."

Then there is the white-haired man who asks us whether
we were enjoying our tour and where we came from, then
spouts a few lines from Goethe's *Faust*[5] in German: "Ahh!
*Deutsch! Augenblick, verweile doch, du bist so schön! Blut ist ein
besonderer Saft. Auf Wiedersehen!*" And he walks around the next
corner, leaving behind two very puzzled travelers.

More poetry comes from Ebrahim, a gaunt electrical engineering student who knows a few lines from Paul Celan's
"Death Fugue."[6] Again two perplexed travelers, this time especially because of his radiant pride during the recital. Ebrahim
doesn't realize that it is all about the Holocaust.

Or Thomas and Mahmut, two physicists from Munich,
whose main objective in traveling seems to be related to smoking vast amounts of hashish. They proudly recount how they
were arrested near Mosul in Iraq for taking photos of a military
base. A couple joints later they send an unusual text message
to Laila: *It might sound odd, but today we both fell in love with you. We
never experienced anything like that before.*

Her reply is just the same as any good wife—silence.

HIKING

We TELL SAEED of our failed attempt at hitchhiking. On a clammy Friday morning he gives us a free lesson. "It's important to explain exactly what you are doing. Don't say that you have no money, but simply say that you always travel like this."

We are standing on a dusty road out of Shiraz. Saeed stops one car after the other by sticking out his arm horizontally. "When someone flashes the headlights while braking it means they're a cab," he explains. "Sometimes I can still convince them to take me for nothing." After about ten stops with drivers all wanting money, we are finally lucky. We are allowed to get in and drive three miles to the start of our hiking tour of Derak, a nine-thousand-foot mountain just outside the city.

We trudge past hardy shrubs and fragile outcrops and signs showing 6,600 ft, then 7,400 ft, and 7,900 ft. Saeed, with a spring in the heels of his worn-out mountain boots, surges ahead, and we wheeze along behind him. It must be eighty-six degrees Fahrenheit, and there's almost no shade on the path ahead. Saeed gives us a rundown on his athletic history. As a child he was interested in gymnastics, moved on to boxing, then kickboxing. "But above all else I love hiking in the mountains because it's not about winning and losing," says the twenty-year-old.

Once he sets his mind to something he takes it seriously. At the moment it is couchsurfing. "If I don't have a guest in three days, I feel lonely."

His big dream is finally to make a few return visits and to travel around the world. To Holland, Germany, and France. To India, Australia, and New Zealand. "But I get my passport only after completing two years' military service, and even then it's still difficult to get visas to most countries." The next problem is money. "Working as a graphic designer I can't put much aside. I'll have to try to find work while traveling."

He used to have a lucrative job selling VPN Internet access for a dollar per month—passwords enabling uncensored use of the Internet: Facebook, CNN, Twitter, the *New York Times*, YouPorn, everything. He rapidly had a couple hundred customers, but then AT&T, the U.S. Internet service provider, blocked the service to Iran, and Saeed couldn't continue.

On top of a small outcrop just below the peak, Saeed spreads his arms and leans back against the now-fierce wind. He tips back his head, closes his eyes, and keeps the pose for a good minute. "Nowhere do I feel as free as in nature," he says.

The ribbons of houses in Shiraz loom beige-colored in the sunlight. "All hail, Shiraz, hail! oh site without peer! May God be the Watchman before thy gate, That the feet of Misfortune enter not here!"[1] hoped Hafiz, who very probably wrote those lines while on a mountain tour.

"I know a German word," says Saeed suddenly.

"Really? Which one?"

"*Spach.*"

"*Spach?* What's that, then?"

"No idea. Doesn't it exist?

"No."

"Oh."

Sometimes all that is needed is a small trigger for what had been serious conversations to descend into utter silliness. Laila and I spend the next half an hour making nonsense sentences with our new favorite word. The definition remains a mystery.

"I'm feeling a bit *spach* today."

"You're looking *spach*, darling."

"Let's speed up. We have to reach the *spach*, and it's pretty late."

Instead of a cross on the summit, there is a hundred-foot-high tower, with a steel stairway and a dome that looks like a giant white soccer ball. It is the core of a weather station that is still at the construction stage. Saeed, with his cheerful disposition, befriends a goatherd and the security guard who is there to ensure that no one is spying or taking photos. "If I didn't have to go to lectures tomorrow, I'd spend a couple days up here, riding donkeys and tending the goats," says Saeed with a glint in his eyes.

"That'd be *spach*," I add.

From: Yasmin Tehran
Hello dear, can you be in Ahvaz on Monday? I found a host there for us. See you soon!

131

"Have you been to Ahvaz?" I ask Saeed on the way back.

"No."

"It's not supposed to be too exciting. Ugly, hot, poor air quality."

"Did you read that in *Lonely Planet?*"

"Yes, it said, 'vast, featureless industrial city.'"

"There are no bad places if the reason you are traveling is to meet people," says Saeed.

How to meet people in Iran

- Choose a lively spot.
- Open up your guidebook.
- Look recognizably lost.
- Wait until someone talks to you (usually takes a maximum of sixty seconds).

THE RED
PERSIAN CARPET

ON MY TRAVELS I was always asking myself how I could repay the Iranians for all the incredible hospitality. On a purely material level I gave them some marzipan (or for devout Muslims some nonalcoholic *shirini* from the candy store), invitations to pay at restaurants (which were sometimes so vehemently rejected that I had no chance), or a couple of cab rides. But all of these seem a bit too meager compared to the experiences that the locals shared with me. They sacrificed time and money, and they even risked problems with the authorities to make my stay as pleasant as possible.

The principle of hospitality is as old as humankind, and in most religions it is considered a virtue. In daily life in Western industrial countries, however, it plays an increasingly minor role. Maybe because religion is losing its importance or because people have become cooler in their social interactions, but probably just because there are fewer opportunities. Mary and Joseph just don't appear at the door asking for a mattress for the night. Also, there is so much infrastructure available for travelers that they no longer need private accommodation.

On the Internet, often criticized as a promoter of social decline, of all places, the ancient idea is celebrating a renaissance. Fourteen million couchsurfers, hundreds of thousands of members of Hospitality Club, BeWelcome, GlobalFreeloaders, and Warm Showers, open their doors to strangers. Some use the portals just as guests, others as hosts. What do the latter get out of it? Often new friendships, exciting stories from travelers, gratitude. But is "What do they get out of it?" even the right question?

In Iran there is another reason for rolling out the red Persian carpet. The people here are hungry for news from other countries, want to know what life is like there. And for some a guest is still an event, a spectacle, because direct contact with people of the same age from Europe, America, or Australia for today's thirty-year-olds is not something that can be taken for granted. "You all look a little bit like people from Hollywood films," an Iranian teenager told me.

In many conversations I felt that I inspired people with my experiences from free countries. Some of them felt motivated to fight for a better future, not to be so apathetic or resigned when dealing with things that they disagree with. If you have comparisons, you can develop aspirations. I'm curious about the effect that growing tourism will have on Iran as ever-increasing numbers of people come here and talk of freedom.

134 I also felt how much good it does to each individual to hear that Iranians are wonderful. Persians are very proud of their country but also know that their country receives bad press throughout the world. Every visitor who shows that he

understands the difference between people and governments does something for the self-confidence of a much-reviled population.

This is also the reason that I have an explicit answer to the question of whether you should visit a country where you are at odds with the political leadership. There are no bad places if the reason you are traveling is to meet people.

NUCLEAR POWER

THE FISHING PORT of Bandar Gaah could be idyllic, a favorite of tourists; it's all there. Two swimming beaches on the Persian Gulf, a couple hundred gleaming white houses, a horse ranch, an old-fashioned pier with creaky wooden boats.

"Those two are mine," says Ahmad, pointing to two sixty-five-foot-long dhows with blue cabins and an Iranian flag fluttering in the east wind. A crew of eight to ten, with two skippers. If the weather is good, they will set off tomorrow for a week. "They usually land about four or five tons of fish, even sharks and tunas," adds the forty-year-old businessman, a muscular guy with a precise part in his hair and a colorful shirt.

Nearby motors rattle. Dark-skinned sailors are redocking two boats. Screws rotate in the water, with black smoke gushing from the funnels. An older man tries to give me a small silver fish that he just caught in the harbor with a nylon line. Reluctantly, he realizes that I really don't have any use at the moment for the creature thrashing about in its death throes on the asphalt.

Ahmad steers his Peugeot from the pier back to the village. Past the "Ashura Square," where, during the month of mourning, *Muharram*, devout Muslims flagellate in public. Past an enclosed playground with brightly colored plastic swings and slides, far and wide not a child in sight. Past some typically Iranian murals on concrete walls of mountains, valleys, and small sailing boats.

"*Privyet*," shouts a motorbiker.

"He thought you were Russian, like most of the foreigners here," explains Ahmad. "Come, I'll show you something." He stops by a green corrugated iron fence separating the beach. Looking through a hole, we can see men and women in bathing suits. In Western bathing suits, that is, shorts and bikinis. "This is the only beach in Iran where men and women can swim together without the women wearing veils," says Ahmad. However, there is a catch—no admittance for Iranians; Russians only. A small concession to foreign workers. The expertise of Russian engineers is so important that they try to make things pleasant for them here.

137

But *pleasant* maybe isn't the right word. There's an awful lot of driftwood and empty plastic bottles lying around. On the other side of the road, directly behind us, there is an anti-aircraft battery and another one three hundred feet away. The Russian beach at Bandar Gaah is probably the securest beach in the world.

On their way to work, the soldiers can peer through the hole, as there are no signs of repairs. "Nothing ever gets repaired here. The government has been planning to completely resettle Bandar Gaah for years, for security reasons," says Ahmad.

He does a U-turn before heading back to the village's second beach, which is no less unusual and begins directly next to the moorings of the fishing boats. The sand is full of plastic garbage, but two children are still swimming. Their parents sit on a blanket, spreading out a small picnic. Relaxed, a perfectly normal Friday at the seaside; there is tea from the thermos and tomato sandwiches.

The reason that this scene, despite its normality, is engraved in my memory has nothing to do with the garbage but what I catch sight of beyond the beach—a gigantic white concrete dome, next to it a minaret-high red-and-white striped chimney with ladders and a square concrete structure. In addition: blocks of houses, looking like a military barracks, and two cranes. Signposts name the facility BNPP, an abbreviation of Bushehr Nuclear Power Plant. The premises is protected by a considerably higher and more solid fence than the Russian beach, naturally without holes but with quite a few watchtowers, guarded by soldiers with machine guns. A thousand megawatt capacity, four cooling pumps, and 163 fuel rods. It is one of the most famous nuclear power plants in the world because it was the very first one in Iran, a milestone in the national nuclear program. Ahmad has to pass the reactor every day when he goes shopping in Bushehr, 7.5 miles away.

"Originally, Siemens was responsible for the construction. In the 1970s there were thousands of Germans living here," he recounts. "But after the Islamic Revolution in 1979, the work was stopped because the political situation was too insecure, and the funding was tricky. The Russians finally finished construction three years ago. I would have preferred a German power plant—then we wouldn't be so afraid of accidents." The government apparently doesn't share these fears. "Five years ago it was decided that all settlements within a three-mile radius of the plant should be relocated, but nothing has happened yet," says Ahmad.

The plans for the construction of another reactor have just been signed, which may speed up this process. Bandar Gaah will die; it is just a matter of time. And then? "I've bought a plot of land in Bushehr. I know where I can go," says Ahmad, but he still finds it sad. He was born in Bandar Gaah, and his parents, in whose garage he now parks the Peugeot, live directly opposite his own one-room apartment.

In the courtyard there are tomatoes and aloe vera plants. Ahmad's nephew has written *Cristiano Ronaldo 7* on the wall. Inside light blue brocade drapes on golden rods hide the windows. The wall is decorated with framed photos of horses, and on the bookshelf there are cups from dressage competitions. Ahmad was for many years a member of the Nuclear Plant Horse Club.

The washroom and showers are outside, and they can only be reached via the courtyard. "I wish I could offer you better accommodation," Ahmad says with typical Iranian modesty, which you have to quickly counter with praise for the quarters. This is not difficult, as many a holiday home landlord on the Mediterranean would give his right arm for such a courtyard, and the room is nothing to grumble about, either. It's just the location that concerns me. It is less than 1,500 feet to the next watchtower. I, too, would have felt considerably better had Siemens built the beige-colored monstrosity.

. . . .

"PLEASE PLAY SOMETHING," says Ahmad, suddenly producing a guitar from next to the sofa.

I strum around a bit, some classical and some flamenco. Ahmad and Laila applaud.

"And now sing something, please."

"I'm not a good singer."

"Doesn't matter, do it anyway." Luckily, Laila has a much better voice. As a duo we wouldn't exactly win on *American Idol*, but we could put on a pretty good performance late nights at a campfire. "Wonderwall" by Oasis, "Good Riddance" by Green Day, "Someone Like You" by Adele. The Iranians love Adele; she could sell 5 million tickets in Tehran if performances by women singers weren't forbidden. Ahmad asks if he could film us on his cell phone. "Please do, but don't show it to all your friends," says Laila.

"Okay," says Ahmad. "You're a great couple."

Not for very much longer, I think to myself. Separation after our ten-day "marriage" is imminent. Bushehr is our last site as a couple since afterward Laila is heading back to Tehran. "I don't believe that anybody feels the way I do about you now," we sing together, and "I hope you had the time of your life," and "I wish nothing but the best for you," and we look at each other and grin because it's all so unintentionally romantic.

We then pass on the guitar to Ahmad. He is a fantastic singer—five times better than us—a strong but also fragile

tenor. He performs "Manoto," which means "Me and You," a
sad love song with a flamenco-like accompaniment. "No, I'm
a bad singer," he says as we express our enthusiasm. "My parents never wanted me to play music. They are very religious
and conservative. When I was young I used to pray five times
a day. I was always in the mosque."

"And nowadays? Not anymore?"

"No, when I was twenty I read a book about an Egyptian physician called Sinuhe and understood that religion only exists
in people's minds. Look at Afghanistan or the Iraq War—can
there be a God when such things happen? Islam creates terror-
ism, and the Iranian government is destroying our country."

"What do you believe in?"

"I believe in human rights, in love, honesty. I hate Islam, but
that is a secret. If I go around saying that then..." He draws
his index finger across his throat. The death sentence awaits all
who renounce the national religion in Shiite Iran.

"I think half of all Iranians are not strictly religious, but the
government is so strong that they have to conceal it. And the
young people are frightened of fighting for their rights because
they know how brutal the *mullahs* are, how many people they
have killed for opposing their views."

The conversation has turned. A few moments before, we
were having a pleasant musical afternoon, and now we are
talking about death, fear, and religion, with Ahmad saying one
forbidden sentence after the other.

I have often experienced such shifts in mood in Iran.
Moments of lightness are more fragile and more precious   141
than elsewhere. A downpour can at any moment drench cheerful small talk at a garden party, even if there were no signs of
clouds before.

In the evening Ahmad says his goodbyes. He plans to stay with his parents and leave us his apartment. He doesn't want to disturb our honeymoon in Bushehr.

At night a relay of red lights illuminate the dome and chimney of the power plant. On. Off. On. Off. I feel like I hear a constant humming coming from that direction, but it might be just my imagination. "I've never seen you so radiant," says Laila. Well, I guess there had to be at least one nuclear power joke. We sit on the couch, drinking tap water. She then draws a spot on my forearm with a pen. "My dad always does it to my mum, just to annoy her. I think it's really cute."

"I think Ahmad thought we were pretty cute, too."

"It's my best marriage so far, but it's also my first." Then she grabs the guitar and starts playing "Nobody's Wife."

Laila gets Ahmad's bed, and I get the mattress on the carpet. We turn out the light. My bus leaves at six in the morning. "It'd be gloriously forbidden to have sex in Iran when not married, wouldn't it?" says one of us.

"Yes, forbidden," is the answer, but she stresses the word in such a way as to make clear she doesn't intend to replace it with "exciting" or "an excellent idea." In a romantic Hollywood comedy this would be the moment when something unexpected happens. In Iran, too. Someone knocks at the door—pretty hard. Not our door but outside near the garage. Always four or five knocks and then silence. We don't dare move. Tourists staying the night so near to a nuclear power plant are automatically thought of as spies, if noticed. And the knocking continues. Laila sits up in bed and slowly puts on her veil as quietly as possible. Our door isn't locked; we have no key. Is it possible that our host has lured us into a trap? Ahmad seems nice enough, but we've only known him a few hours. Paranoia is a mean power that can destroy trust in seconds. We hear steps in the courtyard. A male voice shouts something. More steps. More shouts. But nobody enters. The footsteps fade, and a metal door opens and closes. Then it is so silent that I can hear my own breath.

LOST IN
TRANSPORTATION IV

THE BUS CALLS itself VIP and has red upholstered reclining seats and legroom comparable to a first-class seat on an airplane. The onboard menu consists of orange waffles called *khootka wafer* and date cookies that answer to the name of *kutlu*. And a paper cup with an *Angry Birds* motif and a 10 per cent fruit nectar whose contents include the interesting words *pineapple constantrate*. It comes in a laminated foil pouch with a couple ISO certificates printed on it and a halal stamp but with no instructions about how to open it. A sharpened straw was glued to the outside, which proves unable to pierce the foil. The contents don't seem to be intended for consumption.

After a divorce, a temporary phase of disorientation is nothing unusual. I'm alone again, the wedding ring stowed away deep inside my backpack. After a six-hour journey, the bus spits me out at a roundabout on the outskirts of Ahvaz. Roundabouts are perfectly suited for making you feel lonely. Every driver behind every steering wheel seems to have an objective; I am the only one who has none. I stand here, with my thirty-three-pound backpack, on the fringe of a city. I have no street plan, and I only know that it's hot, it's ugly, and there's no worse place to breathe. In the World Health Organization's list of the world's most-polluted cities, Ahvaz has the first place. In comparison, Beijing, New Delhi, or Tehran are oases of fresh air. Nowhere in Iran is the average life expectancy so low. The city is famous for the orange clouds of smog from heavy industry that cloak the houses in the evenings. To put it another way: people who don't smoke only have themselves to blame, as health-wise there is hardly any difference.

All the traffic signs are in Persian, Ayatollah Khamenei stares down from a number of gigantic posters, and everyone else is staring, too, as tourists here are scarce. My host is working until late afternoon, and I have five hours to kill. The traffic is a wild spectacle of sheet metal and wheels. If you meet people who are too perfect, too nice, and friendly, you automatically look for skeletons in the closet, for some sort of twisted hobby, for something that compensates for this nicer than niceness, something that shows that the person has weaknesses and flaws. With Iranians you don't have to look far. In fact, you just have to go to the nearest main road in any city—their most warped hobby is driving. The second that any Iranian turns the ignition key, he or she forgets ever to have heard the term *taarof*, politeness, and morphs into a fishtailing, honking, fuming Saipa monster in hot pursuit of pedestrians.

I would have loved to have sought safety in a café, even a Starbucks would have been okay, but there are none, only fast-food joints with plastic tablecloths full of crumbs. I know

145

laundromats in Berlin or Hamburg with more charm than the average Iranian hamburger joint. I buy a grilled lump of grouund meat in a bun that has seen better days and just stay there for an hour. What shall I do? I don't even known the direction of the city center. I decide to try an experiment. I go out and wave down a cab. "Imam Khomeini Street," I tell the driver. Every city in this country has a Khomeini Street, usually in the middle.

"Hotel?" asks the driver.

"No," I reply. "City center."

He doesn't understand. With gestures he tries to tell me that Khomeini Street is quite long. I nod and try it with telepathy: just get going and when I like the look of somewhere, I'll tell you to stop. The telepathy doesn't seem to work. Instead, he asks passersby if they can speak English. He asks a bus stop line full of veiled women and a driver in the next lane. Nobody can.

I repeat "Khomeini Street," together with a reassuring gesture intending to convey that it's okay, that I know what I'm doing. Actually, I have no idea what I'm doing. Due to the lack of earthly assistance, the cab driver turns to Allah and starts muttering a prayer. In doing so, every now and then he rests his head on the steering wheel, which, considering the present traffic situation, is clear evidence of his trust in God.

After crossing an arched bridge over the River Karun, a medium-sized river with a color that doesn't inspire much confidence, we seem to be approaching something like a center—inshallah. On the horizon I see the methane gas flares of a number of oil rigs.

The driver brakes and says, "Imam Khomeini" and points to a street on the left that is completely canopied. I would have liked to have given him the thumbs-up sign to say that everything is fine, but I am worried that it could be mistaken for an obscene gesture, so I just pay up and set off.

Sauntering through the world's hottest city, with more than 1 million inhabitants, in the early afternoon with a heavy backpack is not a good idea, but I don't have a better one. The air doesn't actually seem to be too bad, but maybe I'm just lucky, as there is a slight breeze. Photorealistic murals of war martyrs adorn the walls of the houses, and stores sell car parts, household goods, and fruit. A couple youths next to a kiosk ask where I come from. They ask me to take a photo of them with a soccer magazine, then they switch to a sales pitch. One of them gets a pack of pills with *Tamol* xxx and *Made in India* written on it from the space next to a dumpster. He flexes his substantial biceps to show what the pills can apparently achieve and says "illegal." After I turn him down he asks: "Whiskey? My place?" but we still can't come to an agreement.

Instead, I go the *Hoetl Iran*—the huge illuminated sign on the roof has got the letters mixed up—to eat chicken and rice at the restaurant there. The room feels as if it has been cooled down to ten degrees. Vivaldi's *Four Seasons* caresses the ears, 147

and the waiters in white shirts are serving food to the rhythm of "La primavera." The heat-afflicted Ahvazis would presumably love to have four seasons. There is no way that I would have visited the capital of the oil and gas province had Yasmin not suggested it as the starting point for our trip to two battlefields of the Iran-Iraq War.

At five in the afternoon Farshad picks me up in his Peugeot Pars. The slim forty-six-year-old with a mustache has just finished work as an engineer at a thermal power plant. "Welcome to the hottest city in Iran," he says, pointing to the display on the dashboard—107 degrees Fahrenheit. "This is still harmless; in summer it is up to ten degrees hotter."

"How do you survive?"

"By spending as little time as possible outdoors," he says.

Farshad has been to Germany a number of times for energy conferences. He lists the cities: "Frankfurt, Mannheim, Stuttgart, Hamburg." And he even remembers the names of subway stations: Messehallen, Schlump. "They're supposed to be building a subway here, but it is extremely difficult because in some places the oil is only fifty feet below the surface." The natural resources here are enormously valuable, but they are forever causing problems. Soon the airport here will be moved to a site ten miles away because a large amount of black gold has been discovered below the landing strip.

Farshad lives in the Koorosh district, in an expensively furnished apartment that includes a classy leather couch. On the wall there are *Quran* pictures and a painting of a Tuscan landscape and a wooden clock, which every half hour chimes a grotesquely distorted Big Ben melody. He introduces me to his wife, Maryan, and his two children: thirteen-year-old Shayan and eleven-year-old Shaqiba.

The most noticeable resident, however, is a yellow-beaked mynah with gray-black feathers, and the name doesn't remain a puzzle for long, frequently saying "mynah," with a hefty bobbing of the head. In the same way as parrots, mynahs can mimic sounds in robotic tones. Its repertoire, however, includes enough croaks, hiccups, and peeps to supply a number of pinball machines with sound effects. Farshad opens the cage. The bird hops out, then craps on my backpack before hopping onto my head. Still, better than the other way round. "We just bought it ten days ago for 400,000 toman at the bazaar," says Farshad while cleaning my backpack with a tissue. "Watch out for your eyes."

I cover my face with my hands. Being denied a feast of my eyes, the mynah pecks away at my forehead in the hope of finding something edible. This is not the beginning of a wonderful friendship.

The doorbell rings, and Yasmin arrives. Her plane from Tehran landed at the oil field airport an hour ago.

"What have you got on your head?" she asks.

"*Mynaaah, mynaaah,*" croaks the bird in answer.

WAR

AT THE ENTRANCE, next to a huge visitors' car park there is a child's coffin wrapped in an Iranian flag. In front of it are artillery shells, pale red plastic tulips, and a solitary dusty shoe. The wall behind is made of sandbags. A sign states: *Welcome to the place where martyrs went to God*, and the child in the coffin is one. In no other country in the world are so many martyrs revered as here; in every city there are posters of their faces on the streets. On the walls of housing blocks there are paintings of the war heroes, and hundreds of thousands of them rest in the enormous cemetery of Behesht-e Zahra in Tehran.

In this life they are idols, and in the afterlife they have a great time, at least if you believe the promises in the *Quran*. Those who die on the battlefield enter Paradise, regardless of the kind of life they had led up until then. They can expect servants, magnificent houses, and seventy-two virgins at their disposal. Soldiers who were about to be sent into battle were given a plastic key, *Made in Taiwan*, which was supposed to guarantee them quicker access to Paradise. In the firm belief of eternal rewards, human chains of young men walked hand in hand across minefields toward enemy machine gun fire. A number of mines remain on the battlefield of Fath ol-Mobin to this day. Visitors are not allowed to leave the designated trail. Several Iraqi tanks are scattered around looking like huge dead insects, and were it not for the shrubbery, you might think that they had been destroyed yesterday and not thirty years ago.

On September 22, 1980, 100,000 Iraqi soldiers with tanks attacked Khuzestan. Saddam Hussein wanted to seize the oil-rich province because he was convinced of a historical link to Iraq. He was hoping for support from Iranians of Arabic descent, who had long been campaigning for independence. And he was hoping for a victory within a few weeks, as Iran was militarily weak after the fall of the shah. But what followed was the longest war between two countries of the twentieth century, with hundreds of thousands dead on both sides and millions more wounded. In the almost-nine-year war the borders between the two countries were continuously moving with conquests and reconquests.

151

The scenes of the battles are now pilgrimage sites. According to official figures, 3.5 million tourists visited the battlefields in 2013, around 5 per cent of the population. The pilgrims are called "The Passengers of Light." "The state subsidizes almost all the travel costs," says Yasmin, who got her master's degree in this kind of tourism. She is wearing black gloves because it is not considered acceptable to show nail varnish at holy sites. "One week, including full board, one night in a five-star hotel, and a trip to Khomeini's birthplace for twenty thousand toman." A seven-day, all-inclusive patriotic tour for five dollars—an unbeatable offer.

"Citizens are supposed to discover what foreigners did to us," explains Yasmin, which is why film projects on the topic are state-sponsored. More than seven thousand Iran-Iraq War films have been made since 1988; the directors are certain not to make losses. For the government these subsidies are good investments, as the longer the memories of war remain in people's minds, the more certain they can be that they will stay in power. Because the war shows that Allah was on the side of the Iranians, who managed to strike back at a far more powerful nation. Because the grief at the loss of family members is so intense, even today, many people are not prepared to risk their lives or the lives of their children for anything (rebellion against the regime, for example). Because it is always good to whip up hatred for the U.S. supporters of Iraq, and then people more readily blame the archenemy for internal deficiencies than mistakes of their own government.

On the ground in front of the entrance are paintings of the Israeli and American flags, and the latter is so faded that it is hardly recognizable. "Everyone who enters has to tread on them," explains Yasmin. You have to make a detour to avoid them. The choice of the blue Star of David as a doormat is surprising, as during the war Israel supplied antitank missiles and

Uzi machine guns to Iran. The propaganda machinery nowadays doesn't want anything to do with that. For them Israel
was always allied with Iraq.

A former commander of the Iranian troops, who introduces himself as Ali Sorkheh, guides us through the trail of
the memorial. "Everyone should know the truth about the
battlefields," says the muscular fifty-seven-year-old with a
hoarse voice. He is wearing sunglasses, and has white stubble
and "Prima" sneakers. He's been a guide for twenty-three years.
"During Operation Fath ol-Mobin, 3,000 Iranian and 25,000
Iraqi soldiers died here, and 50,000 were captured." And
already, discovering the truth about the battlefields is not as
simple as it seems. His numbers are exaggerated. According to
independent estimates of the Center for Strategic and International Studies, some 5,000 Iranian soldiers died, while 14,000
Iraqi soldiers died or were taken prisoner during Operation
Fath ol-Mobin. Sorkheh picks up a cartridge case. "Saddam,"
he murmurs. "Many of us still have these things in our bodies."

I ask him whether he has any war wounds. "My lungs are
ruined from mustard gas. Germany supplied Iraq with chem-
ical weapons."

The hilly surroundings of clay soils and individual shrubs
seem very dreary, as they consist mainly of two colors, light
brown and green, exactly like the camouflaged tanks of which
only the wrecks remain. As if to add a bit of color, a few places
show posters of mutilated bodies, portraits of teenage martyrs,
or shots of ayatollahs Khamenei or Khomeini next to patriotic
slogans: It was a war of Truth against Lies or The greatest victims are
the families of the martyrs.

Sorkheh shows us a hidden Iraqi bunker. "Exactly the same
kind of bunkers as the Israelis built on the Golan Heights." For

153

him this is evidence that the Israeli military advisers were supporting the Iraqis.

The most striking building on the compound is the "Tomb of the Eight Unknown Soldiers," which is still unfinished—a rectangular mud brick construction with a white tower whose stepped spires look like a ladder to heaven. At the entrance Sorkheh places his right hand on his heart and bows, then goes around laying his hand for a moment on the tombstone of each of the eight graves fixed to the ground in two rows of four. "No identification tags were found for these martyrs," he says. Only the date of death and the battle are mentioned. *Karbala 5, Ramedan, Val Fadj 8. Val Fadj* means dawn, the time when the Iranians began most of their assaults. Yasmin points to a red bandana hanging on the wall.

Ya Hussein is printed on it. "This was the chant before every battle: 'In the name of Imam Hussein,'" says Yasmin. The grandson of the Prophet Muhammad died 1,300 years ago, after being ambushed at Karbala. Every year, during the sacred month of *Muharram*, Shiites mourn their ancient martyr, and Karbala in Iraq is still their holiest pilgrimage site. Hussein is also supposed to be the guardian of the virgin Paradise reserved for victims of war. So, *Ya Hussein* is the Persian variation of *Morituri te salutant*.

When the neighboring countries finally agreed on a ceasefire in August 1988, the borders were exactly as they had been before the war. "The Iraqis built 150 miles of roads in six months in Khuzestan," says former commander Sorkheh. "That was the only good that came out of the war."

The next day one of these roads takes us to the groves of crownless date palms some seventy-five miles south of Ahvaz. Tens of thousands of tree trunks rise skyward, nothing

154

remaining of the crowns but a few charcoaled leaf fronds. They have been there for more than twenty-five years, disfigured, lifeless, like a paralyzed ghost army guarding for all eternity the mud-colored plains of Khuzestan, the most valuable province, but surely not the most beautiful.

"These are the 'trees of resistance,'" explains Yasmin. "Saddam had them all torched because they could have been used as cover by the Iranian soldiers. The trees died but didn't fall, which is why they became a symbol of our fighting spirit and pride. Not one of them has been felled since the war." Martyrs are particularly venerated in Iran, even if they are trees.

Ahmad Mahmoudi drags his left leg; he still has two bullets in his thigh, and he had four in his arm. He knows what it feels like to face a volley of bullets, and the sound of a tank shell exploding a few feet away. It is a miracle that he is still living. The dark-skinned forty-nine-year-old in military uniform is standing on a wooden jetty on the banks of the Shatt al-Arab and talks about the war to a group of more than twenty black-veiled tourists.

The jetty looks as if it were once a ferry terminal, but no ship crosses these waters. The border river Shatt al-Arab was one of the reasons Saddam Hussein invaded Iran. It is Iraq's only waterway to the Persian Gulf and particularly valuable for merchant ships, and he no longer wanted to share this with his neighbors. We are in the town of Arvand Kenar, and looking across the river you can see Iraq, four miles as the crow flies to the town of Faw. We can see a blue mosque dome, transmission towers and minarets, a few old-fashioned dhows. Conspicuous No Swimming signs and steel tank traps ensure that no one gets silly ideas. From the moment of our arrival we notice that our presence is making the soldiers nervous. One

155

asks if he can photograph me. "You are the first non-Muslim visitor here," he says. Then he wants to know what I'm doing here.

"I'm a tourist and very interested in the Iran-Iraq War," I answer. Initially, he seems to be satisfied, but he is never more than fifteen feet away from me and always snapping away on his digital camera.

The most striking exhibits in the open-air war museum are the naval boats and the heavy artillery, and a twenty-foot-long metal tube with a kind of cartoon on it. The colored illustration shows how soldiers made a pontoon out of five thousand such tubes, which was strong enough to carry tanks to the opposite bank. Above it stands a gigantic billboard at least fifty feet wide showing the two bearded Supreme Leaders, Khomeini and Khamenei. It is pointing toward the bank. On it the message WE ARE RESISTING can be read by anyone on the Iraqi side with a pair of binoculars.

156   The Iranians consider it a triumph to have driven back the invaders, even if, in truth, like in most wars, there was no winner.

No one knows the four-mile stretch of water to Iraq better than the veteran Ahmad Mahmoudi. Three armed soldiers form a circle around us as he tells us his story. "I was with the Basij paramilitary volunteer militia. Every night at about ten o'clock I snorkeled to the Iraqi bank to spy out assault targets. Two hours across, two hours back, despite waves and current. The enemy had radar, watchtowers, machine guns, and minefields, and they were armed to the teeth. Our strongest weapon was our belief in God, and we were never noticed. I wasn't afraid; I was prepared to die." Mahmoudi smiles a lot, and he smiles proudly when he is giving his account. He plays the role of war hero perfectly, as he already has done hundreds of times—an ideal person for the job of a line-toeing tourist guide. Behind him, a passenger ship rattles by, full speed to the Persian Gulf, as if trying to leave the former war zone behind as quickly as possible.

"Three to five men went into the water simultaneously, always the youngest, all between fifteen and twenty. I didn't have a beard like this at that time." Every night Mahmoudi swam for his life with a plastic key to Paradise around his neck. Never will he forget the beginning of Operation Dawn 8. "On February 11, 1986, we were two thousands snorkelers. We were the first to land to secure important posts, then came the high-speed patrol boats. We conquered Faw and managed to hold the city for two years and two months."

The war seemed to be turning in favor of Iran. Ayatollah Khomeini ordered the counterattack and wanted to advance to the holy city of Karbala. But the military superiority of the enemy in the end was too much. The units were driven back, and two years later Faw was again in Iraqi hands. Operation Dawn 8 was a pyrrhic victory. But in the long run Mahmoudi thinks Iran did better, and he is pleased that Saddam Hussein is now dead. "Saddam *kodja ast*? *Iran kodja ast*?" he asks. "Where is Saddam now? Where is Iran now?"

The answer to the second question is to be found on the jetty, where Iran stops and the water starts, on a signpost: *Karbala: 375 miles.*

I take a few photos, but Yasmin whispers that it would be better to go. "The soldiers are becoming suspicious; they don't think you are a normal tourist." As a parting gift, Mahmoudi gives us two black-and-white Basij bandanas and kisses me on both shoulders. A soldier is pointing a camera in our direction and seems to be filming us. No one is unfriendly, but I feel that the atmosphere is about to shift. We climb into the car, and our driver puts his foot down. Yasmin casts aside the bandana with an energetic movement.

"I'm annoyed that he didn't mention the navy once. He was acting as if the Basij militia won the battle alone. My father fought here, and he was in the navy."

"Why would Mahmoudi keep it a secret?"

"It sounds more heroic. The Basij were volunteers without military training. If they can defeat heavily armed Iraqi troops, then it's evidence that Allah was on our side."

"What has your father told you about Operation Dawn 8?"

"He was here for more than two years. During an attack, a bomb landed right next to him, and three friends were totally ripped apart. He was luckier, but is deaf in one ear. He calls that his 'souvenir' of the war."

"As a child did the conflict affect you?"

"Up to the age of seven I knew nothing but war. We were always afraid about dad. Once he didn't contact us for six weeks, no sign that he was alive. Then a soldier rang our doorbell and told us that he had been found on a seventy-foot island near Bandar Abbas. He had swum there to avoid advancing tanks, and he had survived for weeks almost solely on

American chocolate. When he came back he had a huge beard and was just skin and bones."

"Was he acclaimed as a war hero?"

She laughs. It isn't a cheerful laugh, but one full of bitterness. "Two years ago he was thrown out of the navy because he wasn't a devout enough Muslim."

Over an evening meal of spaghetti our hostess, Maryan, tells of low-flying jets over Ahvaz. "Saddam's MIGs," she calls them, adding that Iranians always say "Saddam" when they are talking of the enemy, as fundamentally they have nothing against Iraq. "Saddam's MIGs sometimes flew so low that they brushed the treetops, and branches fell to the ground. I had to cover my ears to avoid being deafened." While we are still eating, Farshad releases the mynah from its cage. A screeching bundle of black feathers catapults through the kitchen and uses this sudden freedom to catch up on all the movement that it has been denied in its daylong imprisonment. It hurtles from the sink to the kitchen cabinet, then from the mantelpiece to the table leg, from Yasmin's hair to my feet.

Maryan, despite the distractions, tries to continue her account. "When I was thirteen, in 1983 or 1984, Saddam announced on TV that Ahvaz was going to be bombed at midnight." Conquest of the oil city was a declared goal of the leader. "Hundreds of thousands left the city by foot on the same day, taking with them only gold or money. My father remained at home because he was worried about looters. Luckily, the bombing didn't happen. After a week in a tent, we returned home. Several people died from scorpion or snake bites during this time."

I find it difficult to follow her, and it has nothing to do with a lack of drama in her words. What a tree trunk is for a

159

woodpecker, my foot is for a hyperactive mynah. Continuously it pecks away at my socks with its small beak. Its understanding of the correct food chain seems to be pasta, tourist, bird. Maryan has different ideas and grabs a brush and sweeps the bird aside. Farshad dashes after it. I wonder whether *Angry Birds* was conceived after such a moment. They almost manage to trap it on the table, but my plate is in the way. Spaghetti and ground meat and porcelain plummet to the floor, and the mynah flaps up to a shelf.

"*Mynaaah, mynaaah,*" it goads.

Farshad jives and dives, the bird flaps and flees. After three minutes of hot pursuit worthy of a computer game, the creature is captured and returned to its cage. Maryan gets me a new plate, and I wipe the red Bolognese sauce from the laminated tiles with a napkin.

BACKGAMMON

So LONG AS we are traveling near the border to Iraq, the war doesn't let us go. In Kermanshah, 250 miles northwest of Ahvaz, we are guests of a military friend of Yasmin's father. She contacted him a day ago because no couchsurfers had offered accommodation, and on the spur of the moment he invited us to stay. "You've become fat," says Azim as he hugs Yasmin. He is forty-seven but looks over sixty. Thin hair, melancholic eyes, an emaciated but still muscular body. He is wearing only training pants and an undershirt. He has a tattoo on his right upper arm in Persian lettering done by a fellow soldier, which reads: *Even if I was poor and had no roof over my head, I would never swap my honor for a good meal.*

"*Salam*," I say as a greeting.

"Don't say '*Salam*.' I hate these Arabic words. You have to say '*Dorut*.' That's Persian." Then he apologizes for his simple apartment. "My house is small. I wish I could offer you something better." With his wife, Susan, thirty-seven, and their five-year-old daughter, Azadeh, he lives in a five-hundred-square-foot apartment in a plain apartment block with a sand-colored concrete facade. The stairwell stinks of decaying garbage. "The military pays the rent, so there's no chance of anything bigger," says Yasmin. Azim has been without a job for six months; he is a plumber by trade.

He gathers a few photo albums and opens a pack of Golden Deer cigarettes. The pictures show tanks and smiling men with Type 56 assault rifles, the Chinese variant of the Kalashnikov. Young soldiers with naked chests pose on the beach on the island of Tonb-e Bozorg. Azim was there during his military training. Today he no longer smiles when he talks about the war. "Thirty-six countries supported Iraq." Azim draws the number 36 on his hand with a pen, as if he can only believe it if it is written down. "The Germans and Dutch supplied nerve gas, the Russians tanks, the French Mirage F1 fighters, the Arabians money." He doesn't speak English, so Yasmin translates for me. Little Azadeh clambers onto her father's lap and shows him a picture of an eagle that she has just drawn. He strokes her hair.

On a glass table in the living room there are a couple of apples. Azim picks up one and points to different places as if it were a globe: "Iran. Germany. U.S.A." The green apple looks the same all the way around. "What are we people? Just tiny grains of sand," says Azim.

Then he asks me to cut him an apple in small pieces. To show why he reaches inside his mouth and takes out an artificial lower jaw. "Karbala 5. A tank shell. Landed next to me. Killed some friends, sent stone chipping flying into the air, and one of them hit me in the mouth. Since that day in spring 1987, Azim gets anxiety attacks if there are sudden loud noises. Thunderstorms are hardly bearable. Operation Karbala 5 was the biggest battle of the war: 65,000 Iranians died in an unsuccessful attempt to storm the port city of Basra.

"We're worried about him," says Yasmin. "He is more sensitive than the others, and his lungs are damaged by the toxic gas, but there's no money for treatment. It's good to see him like that with his daughter." The difference between Azim and the two model veterans at the battlefield for tourists is huge, not only because he probably weighs half as much as Sorkheh or Mahmoudi, but also because he doesn't seem to be playing as well-practiced a role. The war ruined him—you can feel that.

Besides that, what he tells us now makes him more of a war hero than the other two. "I was a sniper," he says. "One night we were recceing an enemy camp. One commander, two other soldiers, and me. We saw a couple Iraqis in front of their tents. 'Shoot them,' said my commander. I crawled forward a little, got my rifle into position. Instead of aiming at the men, I set my telescopic sight on one of their weapons, and pulled the trigger. They were startled and jumped up. I waved at them to quickly get lost, and they thanked me with a hand signal."

While we are talking Susan lays a plastic sheet with a tropical island motif on the floor and brings in one delicacy after the other. *Ghormeh sabzi*, a traditional lamb stew with beans and seven herbs, grilled chicken, rice with a typical golden brown crust, and homemade yogurt and salad. In view of this feast I decide never to take the phrase "I wish I could offer you more" seriously again while in Iran.

Azim is no longer as talkative, his gaze often in the distance. Only once, on receiving a text message, does he hint at a smile.

"What's up?" asks Yasmin.

"A friend's just sent me a joke."

"Come on, then."

"It's more a piece of advice. If your car breaks down, jump up on the roof and crap on it. Why? Because Rouhani crapped on Iran and Iran works!"

In backgammon, fifteen black checkers fight against fifteen white checkers. Whoever first bears off the last checker from the home board is the winner. If two or more checkers are on one point, then they are unable to be taken. If one checker is alone on a point it is vulnerable. Black and white, alone weak, together strong—the game, which was invented in Iran five thousand years ago, is a pretty good metaphor of war. "It's 50 per cent head and 50 per cent luck," says Azim, and I ask myself if he would say the same about his war service. He sets up a game on a handmade wooden board. Two checkers on point 1, five on point 12, three on point 17, and five on point 19. He plays against Yasmin, aggressively banging his checkers on the wooden board. Within a few minutes he has effortlessly won three times in a row. "He didn't make a single mistake," says Yasmin admiringly. "Besides, he got doubles slightly more often than me."

. . . .

THE WAR VICTIMS of Kermanshah are buried in a huge soldiers' cemetery. Hundreds, thousands of polished gravestones, like toppled black dominoes on the stony ground. They are roofed, and every roof is shaped like a basketball court. There are at least ten such gigantic roofs. The cemetery is open at the sides. The date of birth, date of death, the soldier's name, and the father's name are written on the gravestones, and most of them have portraits of the victims. Where there are no portraits you can find a stylized dove with wings pointing upward. Its silhouette resembles a tulip, the flower of martyrs. Iranians believe that when a soldier dies in battle a tulip grows from his blood.

Azim stops at a grave. "A cousin of his. He was just seventeen," explains Yasmin.

"All these men. And children. They all died for nothing," says Azim.

A man with a high-pressure cleaner spraying the neighboring mass graves shouts something at us.

"We should go," says Yasmin. "He said if the secret service people see us, they'll arrest us."

Azim begins a discussion, saying that he's a veteran and we are his friends. Then we go back to his Paykan. Two men approach us on a motorbike, stop next to the driver's door, and ask us what we are doing here. Azim repeats that he fought in the war, that he has dead relatives here, that we are his friends, then we drive off.

"During the war, lists were always being distributed with the names of the dead," says Yasmin. "One day Azim's name appeared on one of them. His family gathered at home all

165

wearing black and mourning. The next day they discovered that it was a mix-up."

We drive up to a roundabout near a mosque adorned with a gigantic mosaic Ayatollah Khomeini portrait, then on to a highway leading out of the city. The mountainous landscape all around combines incredibly beautiful nature with incredibly ugly factories.

Often, Azim looks nervously in the rear-view mirror. With every mile he becomes more and more quiet. At the next gas station, however, is the next unpleasant surprise. Gas has become almost 50 per cent more expensive overnight: instead of 2,700 toman a gallon, it now costs 3,800 toman. "The government sets the price," says Yasmin. "If gas becomes more expensive, everything becomes more expensive. Great. Just great."

During the journey Azim tells the story of Farshad and Shirin. I hear it for the second time. We are on the way to Mount Bisotun, where the brave stonemason was supposed to have hewn his tunnel as a token of his love.

We pay for the tickets at a small kiosk—fifteen thousand toman for tourists and two thousand for locals—the usual fee for Iranian attractions. The foreigner tickets are apparently sold out, and the ticket seller tears off eight local tickets to arrive at roughly the right price. Quite a pile of paper, which conveys the feeling of having paid too much far better than mere figures.

The footpath runs below a cliff towering above for more than 3,000 feet. It winds past a 2,500-year-old bas-relief depicting King Darius with captured enemies, hands tied and ropes around their necks, and a statue of Hercules looking strangely apathetic. Both are fantastic works of art impressively rich in detail, but it is a bare cliff face, 600 feet wide and 120 feet high, that attracts just as much attention. Dark vertical stripes show where the rainwater runs off, and a couple of bushes defy gravity. From an overhanging ridge you can see that the wall is not natural but has been hewn out of the rock face with enormous effort. It is called Farhad Tarash and according to legend is the work of the lovestruck stonemason. It does look like an awful amount of work, chippping away more than 52,000 cubic yards of limestone in his attempt at capturing the heart of Shirin. Historians have a less romantic explanation: it was probably intended as the base for a monumental relief but was canceled for reasons unknown.

Today's descendants of Farshad and Shirin wear climbing belts with carabiners: a cheerful couple, roped up, are taking turns at leading the way up the rock face. I'm fairly certain that this is better for their relationship than digging a tunnel through the cliff.

MUSIC

"**WE HAVE TO** go. The others are waiting," says Azim suddenly. He has invited a couple relatives for the evening. The rush, however, doesn't hinder him from serving a round of tea from a thermos at the car. There is an Iranian saying that indicates their understanding of punctuality: if you drown, it doesn't matter if it is in one hand's span of water or a hundred hand spans. So if you are late, being a little later isn't going to make much difference. Still, Azim manages to make up a few minutes by consistently speeding, as far as that is possible with an ancient Paykan. Paykan means "lightning," and it is roughly the same as naming a tricycle a "Porsche." The charmingly angular cars are for Iran what the Trabi was for East Germany or the Ambassador for India. Twenty years ago you hardly saw any other makes, but nowadays they are becoming rarer.

At home various uncles and cousins are sitting in the living room and tuning traditional string instruments: tar, setar, and tanbur. A bottle of Teacher's Highland Cream Blended Scotch Whisky is on the table. It doesn't hold the original contents but homemade raisin schnapps, instead. Burns like fire, but the quality is good. We down it in one gulp from tea glasses, and as if to apologize to the throat and the tongue, we rinse it down with a spoonful of yogurt.

"I will now sing a song for a friend who was killed in the war," says Azim. His cousin, Saeed, a professor of calligraphy with an impressive black mustache, accompanies him on a setar, a three-stringed plucking instrument with a body the size and shape of half a coconut and a long neck. What follows is more of a dialogue than interplay. The passionate smoky voice and the delicate instrument alternate absorbing the themes of the other and varying them. For European ears it is unusual music, as it consists not only of whole note steps and semitones but also quarter tones.

"It's a forbidden song," says Yasmin. "Because it's about the importance of freedom." Azim doesn't hit every tone perfectly, but he dives so deeply into the dream he is singing about that everyone is spellbound. Azim bows to the applause, placing his right hand on his heart. A few minutes later a text comes from the neighbors; they had never realized that he was such a good singer.

"Right, now it's your turn," he says to me. Saeed plays a short melody on the setar and then hands me the instrument. "Slant your right hand and then strum just using your index finger." I fail miserably. He shows me again how to do it, and this time at least it sounds similar. "*Affarin!*" says Saeed. "Great! You've got a good ear! A couple months of master classes, and you'll be a pro."

Iranians love exaggeration. Iranians are wonderful, as are their schnapps and songs of freedom and their secret violations of the law.

The morning after, Azim has a headache and talks of dying. He squats on the floor near the window with one leg at an angle. The curtain is open for the first time. He stares out at the gloomy spring sky and smokes one cigarette after the other, daylight falling on his suffering face. He says a sentence without turning his head, and Yasmin noticeably delays translating it for me. Then she whispers, as if she can't say it loud: "He said: I'm looking forward to joining my martyred friends soon."

She again explains that the nerve gas is to blame for everything, and that he drinks excessively every day. He turns his head to a picture on the wall. It shows an avenue of trees in fall; the path between them is full of leaves, and there is a bright light at the end of the avenue. His eyes return to the window and seem to be fixed on a point in the distance. "They all died for nothing," he says.

SMUGGLERS

THE CAB DRIVER taking us to Paveh looks like Mick Jagger at thirty, and the MP3 player is blaring Modern Talking. Compared to last night's music, this is how a screaming hangover feels compared to enjoying an eighteen-year-old single malt.

"Did you know that Modern Talking come from Germany?"

"Really? I learned English from their lyrics," answers Yasmin.

"Then your English is surprisingly good."

"Don't you like Modern Talking?"

"I can think of two hundred German export products that I'm more proud of."

"They're famous in Iran."

The Mick Jagger behind the wheel, who is actually named Farsad, joins in: "We have to listen to singing *mullahs* every day. Compared to them, Modern Talking sounds good." An interesting point.

Despite this, he shuffles to another singer, Hayedeh, a Persian cross between Maria Callas and Adele. "If you're looking for me, I'll be in the bar, and drinking and talking to God," she sings. The lyrics remind me of Hafiz, who also managed to connect the pleasures of alcohol and divine experience. But even without such provocative words Hayedeh would be banned in Iran—women are not allowed to sing alone because the rulers fear it might give men stupid ideas. Shortly before the revolution in 1979 she emigrated to Los Angeles, where she was able to write her songs and record her albums without fear of censorship. "After a concert in January 1990 she had a heart attack and died at age forty-seven," says Yasmin. "The funeral was followed by millions on TV, and all Iranian businesses were closed for the day."

I am relieved to see that Yasmin prefers this music to German pop of the 1980s, and she passionately sings along (of course that is also forbidden, and it seems to irritate our driver somewhat).

If you want to recreate the beauty of a cab ride through wild Kurdistan you should type "Hayedeh Zendegi" into YouTube, shut your eyes, and imagine an adventurous, winding road over a pass between snowcapped mountains and gas trucks and kebab stands on the roadside, with shepherds in baggy pants and stone walls with paintings of patrol cars and scenic views of the Iranian plateau and villages that seem to have been slapped onto the steep mountainside. Houses are built like steps, so that the flat roof of one acts as part of the foundations of the neighbor above.

Border trade must be immensely important for the settlements in the Paveh region; otherwise, no one would come up with the idea of building villages on such steep slopes. We see many military outposts painted in camouflage colors with No Photo signs hanging on the walls. With their rounded towers they remind me of desert forts from the Middle Ages. They are not only important to the government because of the proximity of the border, but Tehran also feels uneasy about the Kurds, as many of them dream of independence. The skies are gray, and it is drizzling a bit.

"I love rain," says Yasmin. She jiggles her shoulders in time with the music and clicks her fingers.

"When you move to Germany you will think differently," I say.

"Definitely not. It's so refreshing. Azim's neighbor named his daughter Baran, which means 'rain.'"

"Poor girl."

"I don't understand you. There's plenty of sun, and you just sweat the whole time."

"The Germans are so crazy about the sun that they produce happiness hormones at the smell of suntan lotion."

"You're weird. Try wearing a veil the whole day in the heat here."

"Which sky color is more beautiful: blue or gray?"

"Definitely gray."

"You're weird, too."

From: KOREK
Welcome to Iraq. Feel at home while you roam on
Korek Telecom network. For inquiries please call
+9647508000411

The Kurd village of Nowsud with 1,500 inhabitants is so close to the border that our cell phones connect to an Iraqi network. We stop for a kebab. On the main street some riders approach, hooves clattering on the asphalt as they gallop. Mustached men in white trousers, using heavy dust-coated cloths

173

for saddles and no stirrups, stretch their legs forward for balance. Some of them have one or two horses or mules behind them on lines, fully laden with bags and bundles beneath their saddlecloths. If most of them weren't wearing Adidas sneakers, I would feel transported back a hundred years.

"Smugglers," says Yasmin. "They go up in the mountains at night and cross the border. The police know all about it, but for a little baksheesh they turn a blind eye."

"What do they bring?"

"Alcohol, cosmetics, household goods, all sorts of things that you can't get here."

"Do you think I can photograph them?"

"Sure."

I go to the roadside, pressing the shutter button time and again; the men are simply too decorative to ignore. Yasmin, too, takes some snaps on her cell phone. One stops and asks whether we are from the government. Yasmin says we are just tourists. "Then you can take as many photos as you want." A soldier with a machine gun wanders around in the middle of the caravan, so the problems with the government don't seem to be too serious.

Judging by what is on offer at the market stalls, the smugglers bring stuff across the border that you can easily live without. Or maybe the goods that arrive by horseback obtain a special aura that makes them irresistible. Okay, they do sell food processors, vacuum cleaners, and pots and pans, which could be useful. But they also offer soap with extract of snakes and snails that's supposed to be good against acne, "Green Berlin Tea" with a picture on the label of what looks like an Indian plantation, with veiled women pickers in front of the Brandenburg Gate. And *Star Wars* characters as garden gnomes.

THE POLICE

OUR TOUR ENDS with two men in traditional Kurdish costumes, who introduce themselves as policemen and ask to
see our passports. You would think that at a market specializing in illegal products they would have something better to do,
but that of course is a very European viewpoint. In the East
the coexistence between racketeers and law enforcers allows
for considerable diversity.

They certainly don't look like public servants: one of them
is wearing a khaki shirt, the other a pink shirt. I am immediately alert. In Kurdistan there are fraudsters who pretend to be
policemen to swindle tourists. You can get a lot of money for
a European passport on the black market because they can be
used to escape from Iran—at least if there is some resemblance
to the rightful owner. So before traveling they would need to
go to a hairdresser to match the hair style and color.

I would love to help refugees, but I need my passport
myself. So I lie and tell them it is in my hotel. I show them a
photocopy of my passport that I always have on me. The larger

of the two men, the guy with the khaki shirt, takes the sheet and shakes his head. "Get in," he says, pointing at Farsad's yellow taxi. He sits on the passenger seat, and his colleague climbs into a silver Peugeot 405 that I hadn't noticed until then. Two soldiers with machine guns are sitting on the back seat of the Peugeot. So they really are policemen.

The police station, whose gate we pass through five minutes later, also looks real. We are led to the entrance. In the courtyard there are two Toyota pickups, and an armed guard patrols the roof, his right thumb on the rifle sling, his left hand fisted behind his back. One of the soldiers tells Farsad that he should reprimand Yasmin for showing her hair beneath her veil. Farsad obeys, but it was not necessary. Yasmin, who was walking right next to him, had already taken the hint.

We are then taken to the interview room. All backpacks are searched. The "Bad Cop" and the "Good Cop" start questioning us. We tell them lots of lies, and I hope that no one notices that the tea cup in my hand is shaking. Finally, the brawny official scrutinizes my camera. He scrolls through the pictures I've taken in the last couple hours. A rider on a horse. Two riders on two horses. One rider with three horses. I must have appeared to him like a Japanese tourist in New York, indiscriminately holding the camera in front of passersby and snapping just because they look American.

"Why so many pictures of riders?"

"We don't have costumes like this; they're magnificent. Anyway, I have to take a lot of pictures when people are moving to get one that isn't blurred," I answer truthfully. If this were a German police station, I might have added, as a watchful citizen, that an occasional glance under the saddlecloth might be interesting. At a German police station I would be fairly sure that nothing nasty would happen—the rule of law will sort it out. I haven't robbed or killed anyone. In a country where after a traffic accident people prefer to sort things out among themselves and no woman would dream of going to the police after being raped, things look different. Where are the lines between amateur photographer and spy, between naive holidaymaker and alcohol-consuming criminal? If "Khaki Man" scrolls further he will find pictures of Azim's whiskey bottle, of the battlefields of Ahvaz, of the nuclear power plant at Bushehr. Then there will be some answering to do.

But he stops scrolling. After 250 pictures of riders, even the hardest cops become tired. Allah bless the smugglers and their horses. He passes my camera back. He finishes his handwritten report and fetches an inkpad, and I sign the report with a print of my right index finger. We are free, and being free feels pretty damn good, in Iran more so than elsewhere.

"I was scared shitless," says Yasmin, as we sit in the taxi. "Luckily, they didn't find the battlefield pictures. Those guys weren't particularly bright."

"Have you often been questioned by police?"

"Of course. Once they questioned me about the BDSM group. I had to show them all my e-mails and Facebook posts, very private stuff. That was nasty. But they released me in the evening."

Our destination for the night is Hajij, and we arrive at dusk. From an aerial perspective the village is shaped like a crescent moon, from the side like a series of steps. Blocks of red stone houses nestle on the slope like oversized rows of amphitheater seats, and there are people on every rooftop terrace, watching people observing other people on other rooftop terraces, or the cows being driven to their stalls, or the Sirwan River flowing

178

in the valley below. Grandmas and grandkids, mothers and fathers—the whole village seems to be on its feet, a wonderful atmosphere. We ask about accommodation and are shown a simple room. A carpet and a socket are the only furnishings. In front of the door there is a mulberry tree. I lodge with Farsad, the cab driver. Yasmin gets a room of her own.

To: Mona Hamedan
Hi Mona, thanks for your message on cs! I might go to hamadan the next days—do you have time to meet or could you even host me for 1 night? Would be great! Cheers, stephan

From: Mona Hamedan
Stephan how old are you? Are you alone? Or coming with your wife?

When in Hajij do as the Hajijs do, so up to the roof it is. Of course, we are immediately invited to tea on one of the public balconies. The women wear long red robes with delicate floral designs. The men have mustaches that would make American actor Sam Elliott turn green with envy, and old men move about with carved walking sticks with rounded handles. Compared to the people here the smuggling riders were wallflowers. In ten years, buses full of Japanese tourists will come to Hajij.

The tea donor, in a gray Kurdish overall, introduces himself as Moharram and is a kind of village elder. He gets his wife to bring a second and third round of hot drinks from the apartment, and afterward a delicious ash soup made from chickpeas, lentils, and spinach.

179

"Why are Iranians so incredibly hospitable?" I ask Yasmin.

"Possibly because at some time in their lives they've had bad experiences with their compatriots but never with foreigners," she suggests and laughs.

"In Germany it's the other way around. According to surveys, it is precisely the places where there are fewest foreigners that hostility toward foreigners is greatest."

We are interrupted as Moharram tells us about his village. "Thirty years ago there wasn't a road here; you could only reach us on horseback," he says.

"Do people here ride to Iraq to smuggle back goods?" I ask.

"No, we are over an hour away from the border. But it's a lucrative business. You can earn 300,000 toman per person per night." That is about seventy-five dollars. In Hajij there is little work, which is why he is hoping for more tourists.

"A few people have found jobs on the construction site of the Daryan dam project."

"Which project is that?"

"They are damming up the Sirwan River. In two or three years the water will rise in the valley. The lower rows of houses will have to go. In earlier days there were two hundred houses here, and soon it will only be half that amount."

"Why do they need the dam?"

"To improve irrigation of the fields, and a power plant is in the planning. On top of that, less water will flow to Iraq. But the construction project has one big disadvantage."

"Which is?"

"A couple years ago Hajij was famous for being a completely nonsmoking village. Even TV teams came here to make reports about us, but after the construction workers arrived, almost everyone started smoking."

The muezzin of Hajij calls to prayer at a quarter past eight. He warps the sound a bit, and a slight echo reverberates from the semicircular village.

"Ten times better than Modern Talking," I say to Farsad.

From: Mona Hamedan
Why don't you answer?

To: Mona Hamedan
I'm 34 and I'm coming alone. Is that ok for you?

From: Mona Hamedan
yeah it's ok, are you married or single?

The next day we reach the last point of our shared travels, one hundred miles farther on, in the town of Marivan. Yasmin will take the night bus from here to Tehran, and I had planned to travel on to Isfahan until Mona from Hamedan contacted me after hearing that I was in Iran from a couchsurfing forum.

She sent me her cell phone number and on the spur of the moment invited me to visit Hamedan. Her profile shows a Middle Eastern beauty in a low-cut black dress and quite a lot of lipstick. I immediately see through the attempt of manipulating male viewers with such imagery, and it leaves me completely cold. But I do intend to stick to my plan of letting the natives influence my choice of route.

To: Mona Hamedan
I'm single, what about you?

From: Mona Hamedan
Ok no problem im 22 & i'm single too:) can you send your
pic for me now? I wanna see you.

The sections of my brain responsible for emotions are happy with the dialogue. The somewhat smaller sector, where "logic" and "keeping a cool head" reside, not so. An attractive woman who doesn't mess around—there has to be some catch. In a movie when a spy smells a trap, he doesn't let his counterpart know it. I feel pretty reckless on sending the requested photo because I'm behaving as if I think everything is beyond suspicion.

How to flirt in Persian

- *Dooset daram*: I love you.
- *Zanam mishi?*: Will you marry me?
- *Jigareto bokhoram*: I want to eat your liver (an expression of great affection).
- *Khoshgele*: beautiful woman

THE PRINCE

OUR HOST IN Marivan, Ehsan, wears a polo shirt and designer jeans, and turns out to be a passionate winemaker and a Persian prince.

"Have you been to Shiraz? The castle in the middle? My great-, great-, great-, great-, great-, great-, great-, great-grandfather Karim Khan Zand lived there. He is a descendent of the Iranian ruler of the late eighteenth century."

"Stephan wants to be the Shah of Persia," says Yasmin. I had almost forgotten our bit of fun in the Golestan Palace in Tehran.

"Then I will have to kill you," says Ehsan. "How about two droplets of poison in the ear, like in *Hamlet?*"

The prince has style; you have to give him that.

"I would like to try some of your wine first," I say fawningly.

"I'll get it later," he says. "You can count yourself lucky; it's the best wine in western Iran. We make 160 gallons a year. But I have to teach you one rule."

"Sure, what is it?"

"When I say, 'What time is it?' the right answer is: 'Wine o'clock.' Can you remember that?"

"Sure. Can I take a shower?"

"You can save your energy. Islamic traditions state that it's customary to wash the body directly after death."

"Oh."

"Nonsense! Of course you can shower."

He drives to the city and returns two hours later with a four-pint plastic container filled with a dark red liquid. "What time is it?" he asks.

"Seven thir… er… wine o'clock!" I answer, and he flashes a satisfied grin. I don't know the other wines of western Iran (there are rumors of a wine-making facility near Urmia, producing beverages just for the diplomatic service in Tehran), but this is pretty damn good. Dry, fruity, a slight hint of blackberries. The aftertaste, however, is a bit furry, and my gums feel numb.

"The first sip always gives me a bit of a jolt," says Ehsan and refills our glasses. "Now each of us could get eighty lashes as punishment."

"What does the winemaker get?"

"Four years in prison per gallon. That would be 640 years for me."

"Even for princes."

"Even for princes. Did you know that it's very easy to mix poison into a bitter drink, like wine?"

"No, I hadn't really thought about it."

He looks rather theatrically at his wristwatch. "You have about two hours—that'll give you time to think about it."

"Hey, the thing about my shah ambitions was a joke. You can have the job."

"Too late."

From: Mona
I saw our piC now i remember you from your profile
stephan, you look awesome and cute:-)

Dying with a love note from a mysterious beauty in my
hand would be a bit too Shakespearean, so I decide to survive the drink. Or did Ehsan sprinkle the antidote into the
next glass of wine, or the one after that? We chat for many
hours, and the prince proves to be a highly intelligent con-
versationalist with a devastating sense of humor, aristocratic
self-confidence, and impressive expertise in illegal indulgences.
("The best hash comes from Karaj, near Tehran, and it's four
times as strong as what Europeans call hash.")

It is one of the many days of my trip that I wish I weren't
always on the move, traveling from one host to the next but
instead staying a little longer, getting more than just a fleet-
ing insight into the lives of others. There is never enough time
for the beginning of a real friendship, but that's the kismet of
backpacking nomads. On the plus side, a whole range of new
short-term friendships are waiting in the future, the online illu-
sion of an almost endless availability of human contacts.

As a leaving present, Ehsan fills a water bottle with the forbidden grape juice. "For the road," he says.

To: Mona Hamedan
Merci! Now its your turn to send me a picture

From: Mona Hamedan
I don't have piC on my phone you can go to cs & see my profile piC

To Mona: Hamedan
That pic is beautiful see you soon!

From: Mona Hamedan
Thanks dear, but i have some acne on my skin, & i don't
remove my eyebrow now because my cousin passed away
& i should stay til the 40th day of her dead after that i go to
beauty salon & remove my eyebrow;)

I like the detailed description of her eyebrow problem. It
no longer sounds like a ploy but rather very human insecurity. Human insecurity is much more preferable, if I have the
choice, than the feared mafia-like prostitution ring luring innocent foreigners via an online travel portal. So I decide to go to
Hamedan the next day—it's on the route to Isfahan, anyway.

From: Unknown Number
Hey.how r u.i m shahin.hamedan c.s. And Mona cousin.
whan u arrive to hamedan?Mona coudent host u.i will host
how many day?

To: Shahin
I will arrive tomorrow. Would be great if you could host me
for 1 or 2 nights! Thanks and see you soon!

LOVE

WOULD BE GREAT *if you could host me,* I write back to Shahin. A very diplomatic answer. The prospect of staying with someone who I know nothing about doesn't appeal to me. My suspiciousness has returned. After a two-hour ride in a Savari cab I'm standing in the middle of Hamedan at a roundabout with a huge stone relief of soldiers and Ayatollah Khomeini. I'm having doubts about whether this stopover was a good idea. Shahin doesn't initially succeed in improving my mood. At first he tells me on the phone to wait for him at Khomeini Square. Then he calls again: "Take a cab, call me back, and give the driver the phone." And two minutes later: "Stay where you are. I'll come and get you."

He doesn't seem to trust me to get into a cab alone. This is typical Persian concern and is well-meaning. You feel like an honored guest but one who is four years old and incapable of performing the simplest of tasks alone. There is a fine line between being helped and being mollycoddled. Every expat Iranian on returning to visit the family for a couple weeks can tell you a thing or two about it.

A casual young man in stonewashed jeans and leather sandals gets out of a cab and greets me with three kisses on the cheek. "Welcome to Hamedan," says Shahin and takes my backpack.

We travel north, changing shared cabs three times. He studies engineering sciences in Isfahan and Kashan. Just the day before, he returned from a fortnight in Iraq, where he worked as a welder. His most recent guests came from Düsseldorf, Bern, and Turkey. We get out of the cab at Juraqan, a suburb near the airport.

Shahin has parked his small decrepit Honda CG125 here. The headlamp seems to have been ripped off, and the speedometer has been attached to the handlebar with a makeshift piece of white cable. "It's already had quite a number of accidents," he explains and indicates that I should get on. We rattle off along a dusty road with dusty stores, stopping at a door to a courtyard. "We used to keep sheep here, but now it's only chickens," he says. I notice that he belongs to the small group of people who spend more time smiling than not. The house consists of a central living room, with doors leading to a kitchen and two other rooms. His room is simply furnished with a desk, a cupboard, and a carpet, with pants hanging on various hooks on the walls. "My mother and brother also live here, but they are away at the moment."

"Is Mona your cousin?" I try to delicately introduce a more interesting subject.

"Yes, she speaks the best English of all our family," he says, adding: "Are you religious?"

Change of subject unsuccessful. "Not particularly. And you?"

"I don't like the Sunnis because they kill people, and the Shiites only believe in dead martyrs. I am Zoroastrian, but it's my

Love

secret. If the government finds out about it..." he makes the international sign for beheading. Death sentences for apostates, though, are rarely carried out. People who are charged simply have to acknowledge their Shiite belief in front of the court and can continue to live. Zoroastrians, as representatives of Iran's ancient religion, can expect a greater degree of leniency than followers of other religious persuasions. More than three thousand years ago they were the first to incorporate concepts like good and evil, God and the Devil, Heaven and Earth in their beliefs, thus inspiring Christianity, Islam, and Judaism.

Shahin suggests an outing. "Dumb idea," I think and say: "Great idea!"

Directly behind the house is a dirt track leading to a hilly field. We ride on the motorbike to a sports hall, where Shahin's friend Parvis works as an equipment manager, another radiant sunshine boy. We drive a little more to go flower picking. Three men on one motorbike, with me in the middle—that is more bodily contact than I had expected for the day, still not exactly what I was hoping for. Flower picking. That's right, you've read it correctly. Shahin and Parvis are passionate flower pickers. I, however, once had a fun-free vacation job in a garden center. Even if there weren't a fair maiden gazing at me longingly from the battlements, like long ago the beautiful Gordafarid entranced the warrior Sohrab, I still could not get any pleasure from picking flowers.

Shahin points to a field full of lilac-colored blossoms. "Saffron. For two pounds I can get forty dollars." So we start picking saffron. A lot of saffron. And a flower that sounds something like "Kalam Kashi." "Good for the heart and good against Alzheimer's disease." Kangar also grows here, a plant

189

with mean spikes in its leaves, and Shahin wears gloves when picking it. In its stem there are milk-colored fibers that you can eat. They taste of nothing.

"Mona doesn't understand why we love Juraqan so much," says Shahin, who hasn't understood that I like Mona very much. Every hour a little more so. Psychologists call this the Romeo and Juliet effect: the greater the barriers to a relationship, the stronger the affection.

To: Mona Hamedan
Hey, how are you? I arrived at shahins place. what is your plan for today?

From: Mona Hamedan
Hi stephan, you and shahin after dinner come to our house & then we going out:)

Things that I find less interesting than meeting Mona on a spring afternoon in western Iran

- Wandering around a bazaar.
- Getting to know a friendly stationer who wants to invite me home.
- Attending the opening of a carpet business.
- Squashing myself between two singing flower-power fans on a motorbike.
- Getting to know a friendly car mechanic who wants to invite me home.
- Photographing Shahin in front of a nondescript stone gate ("for Facebook!").
- Getting involved in a fight (almost) because an obviously drunk teenager wants to relieve his aggression.

- Getting to know a friendly confectioner who wants to invite me home.
- Watching the TV news (Rouhani promises better working conditions, Rouhani wants more exports, Rouhani stresses the peaceful usage of nuclear power).
- Picking saffron.

• • • • • • • • •

"A FRIEND HAS just called me. Do you feel like playing soccer tonight with a couple people?" asks Shahin. My thoughts extend the list to include playing soccer.

"I would rather meet up with Mona," I venture.

"Oh, okay, then we'll have to wait for my brother to get us in his car."

A couple hours later. I might have realized earlier that I was having a date, had Mona's mother, two sisters, a nephew, a cousin, and from time to time also her father, an uncle, an aunt, and her brother not been sitting on the expensive furniture in the living room. Maybe then there wouldn't even have been any need for the memorable appearance of a mysterious relative.

But let's start at the beginning. Mona looks different from her profile photo—dark hair tied in a bun, eyes like black pearls,

191

casual jeans, exceptionally pretty. Her eyebrows don't seem to be out of the ordinary, but maybe as a man I'm missing the analytical eye. With great composure she introduces me to her family members, then places me next to Shahin and seats herself next to her mother. On a flat table there are gherkins, kiwi fruit, and unfortunately, a blunt knife, ensuring that conversing and peeling at the same time is a real challenge.

"They're pretty rich," whispers Shahin and points at the huge Persian carpets. "Each of those cost 3 million toman," $750. So, a good catch.

Mona has one brother and eight sisters, and most of them are married and no longer live at home. She likes Shakira but finds rock music too loud. Her major at university is economics, and today she had a midterm exam in electrical technology (very good); otherwise, at the moment, she has to review for a couple English tests.

"What are you passionate about?" she asks suddenly.

"Travel and music," I reply after a moment of hesitation. "And you?"

"I want to be a dentist," she says, with little passion in her voice. "Or an English teacher. Or a singer."

I tell them about my trip—in the meantime the number of my stops usually triggers a certain admiration—and show them my travel photos on my camera.

"I can say something in German: *Iesch liebe disch!*" says Mona. Conversation meanders along lightly and cheerfully. People come and go, and I notice that Mona often changes places. Sometimes she sits next to me, then gets up to move to one of her sisters, strangely enough, always seconds before a male relative enters, almost as if she has second sight. It is a mystery how she does it.

Her mother is the only woman in the room with a headscarf and smiles at me beatifically the whole time. Her father, however, is a tough guy, a retired haulage contractor, a hat-wearing Persian Sean Connery. Most of the time he is withdrawn, and then suddenly he poses an avalanche of questions: "What do you think of Iran? How much did your camera cost? How much do you earn? What do you do? How much does a laborer earn in Germany? Why haven't you made any effort to learn Persian?"

I'm not too upset when he says goodnight and goes to bed. Shortly afterward a man strolls in, introducing himself as Mona's cousin and saying that he lived in France for a number of decades. He looks to be in his mid-forties.

"*Parlez-vous français?*" he says, suddenly changing the language.

"*Oui, un petit peu,*" I reply. Four strenuous years at school and a long time ago. He sits down next to me, where seconds before his entrance Mona was sitting.

"*Ça va?*"

"*Ça va bien, merci!*"

"*Tu aimes l'Iran?*"

"*Oui, l'Iran c'est magnifique.*"

"*Il y a quelque chose je veux te dire.*"

"*Oui?*"

"*C'est un petit peu compliqué.*"

"Okay."

"*Ma cousine t'aimes bien. Qu'est-ce que tu penses?*"

"*Ah oui? Err… je suis très heureux.*"

"*Mais c'est l'Iran. Il est compliqué. Beaucoup de restrictions. Tu comprends?*"

"*Oui.*"

193

First I think he just likes speaking French, but really he just needs a secret language to use in front of the family gathering. A puzzling character. He gets up and goes toward the door, but Mona intercepts him for a short whispered exchange. The living room is big enough to be out of earshot.

Cousin exits, brother Ali enters. People are exiting and entering at such a rate that I feel like I'm at the theater. Ali is a fairly coarse character who likes to be the center of attention and conversation. One of his sisters brings him some rice and chicken, and she also places a portion in front of me, although I'm not hungry and my "No thanks" was misunderstood as politeness and ignored. Ali is a noisy eater and talks with his mouth full. "Come on, lets meet a few friends," he suggests. Shahin has already begun to say his goodbyes, and also to Mona. Oh, I see. This is going to be a male-only outing, of course. If my host is going, I can't possibly remain here. So much for the *then we going out:)* plan from Mona's text message.

Things that I find less interesting than spending more time with Mona on a spring evening in western Iran

- Racing through the darkness in Shahin's car.
- Watching Ali crumble the tobacco from two cigarettes onto a piece of cardboard, add some crumbs of hash and then skillfully suck the mixture back into the empty cigarette shells.
- Listening to Persian trance music at club levels during the drive.
- Meeting Sanjan, Puya, Mohsen, and Arash.
- Circulating hash cigarettes in a park.
- Answering questions about Bayern Munich, Adolf Hitler, and the going rates of Hamburg's prostitutes.

- Learning a few Persian swear words in return.
- Gazing at the lights of Hamedan from a vantage point on a hill.
- Eating melons at home, at 3:30 AM.

· · · · · · · · · ·

To: Mona Hamedan
Good morning my dear! It was wonderful to meet you yesterday! whats your plans for today?

From: Mona Hamedan
It was a pleasure to meet you too! Tomorrow i have midterm in english institute.i'm studying english like always:)

Shahin is a great guy and a wonderful host. I can't blame him for anything. But he is also a possessive host. The next day we drive to an old-fashioned village to picnic and drink schnapps under a walnut tree. A nice tour, but I'm not so happy about the feeling that I have no say in the planning of our day. On the way home we visit yet another waterfall at the foot of Alvand Mountain, where there is a cable car to the peak.

"This is where young couples come when they want to be alone and grope each other," says Shahin chattily. "The moral police don't come here." Boulders and trees offer the necessary screening.

From: Mona Hamedan
Where are you now?

To: Mona Hamedan
Near Alvand mountain, did you finish studying?

Shahin asks whether I want to drive to a friend's to smoke a hookah. I only have a few hours left in Hamedan; my night bus departs at ten. "It would be much nicer to meet up with your cousin again," I say. He doesn't say anything at first, but on the way home he stops in front of the family apartment. We gather Mona and her sister, and the four of us take a sightseeing tour. And lots of photos. At the grave of Avicenna, the most famous doctor and thinker of his time, nowadays known from the best-selling novel *The Physician*. At a stone monument in the shape of a missile nosecone, in front of a mosque, and at a mausoleum.

"You have beautiful hair," says Mona.

"Can you get me a German girlfriend?" asks Shahin, who seldom leaves my side. Up to the time the three drop me off at the bus stop I am never alone, or even nearly alone, with Mona. Yesterday the extended family, and today sister and cousin. This country is run not only by state surveillance systems but also familial ones. I ask myself how it is possible for people to fall in love and marry under these circumstances. Or do Iranians marry first and fall in love later? Fall in love at high speed? I need to do more research on that.

NEWS

VIENNA—HOPE OF A breakthrough in the Iran nuclear talks: the P5+1 group and Iran are confident that the conflict, which has been smoldering for ten years, can be resolved by the summer. However, the joint statement of the Iranian minister of foreign affairs, Mohammad Javad Zarif, and the high representative of the Union for Foreign Affairs and Security Policy/vice-president of the European Commission, Catherine Ashton, warns that "there is a lot of hard work necessary to overcome differences."

Tehran—After clear criticism of the human rights situation in Iran by the European Parliament, Tehran retaliates. "This declaration is worthless and deserves no attention," says Iran's chief justice, Sadeq Larijani, to officials in Tehran. "It demonstrates the arrogance of the West." Additionally, he accuses the European Union of spreading promiscuity and homosexuality in Iran.

Washington—The planned appointment of Hamid Aboutalebi as Iran's new UN ambassador has created an uproar.

The Iranian diplomat is thought to have participated in the Iranian hostage crisis in 1979. On Thursday, the U.S. Congress unanimously passes a bill denying Aboutalebi a visa.

Vienna—As a reaction to a report of the International Atomic Energy Agency (IAEA), the U.S. has again relaxed sanctions against Iran. A total of $450 million will soon be made available, according to a spokesperson from the U.S. Department of State. The IAEA announced that Iran had, up to now, honored the Geneva interim agreement of last November. The stocks of weapon-grade enriched uranium have been reduced, and the country has, in the meantime, diluted or converted to uranium oxide 75 per cent of its inventory. "Everything is going to plan," said a diplomat.

Noshahr—In Iran a young man escapes execution by seconds. According to a report from the Islamic Republic News Agency (IRNA), the condemned man already has the noose around his neck as the mother of the victim forgives him. He had been condemned to death because during an argument he stabbed the woman's son to death in the city of Noshahr. After China, Iran is the country with the most executions in the world. In 2013, according to official information, 369 people were executed. Amnesty International, however, believes that there were at least a further 335 executions.

Tehran—Blocking the messaging app WhatsApp has triggered a dispute between the government and censorship authorities. "The government is firmly against the ban," says Iran's Communications Minister, Mahmoud Vaezi, to the state news agency IRNA. Previously, the head of the judiciary filtering committee, Abdolsamad Khorrambadi, was quoted as saying, "The reason for this is the adoption of WhatsApp by the Facebook founder Mark Zuckerberg, who is an American Zionist."

London—Journalist Masih Alinejad has created a Facebook page inviting Iranian women to post photos of themselves without a headscarf. The feedback is enormous, and within a couple days hundreds of photos are posted on the site, attracting thousands of likes. Alinejad lives in exile in London, having been forced to leave her country after exposing a corruption scandal.

Tehran—Many people demonstrate in front of the Ministry of the Interior in Tehran for "chastity and moral security." They are protesting against any softening of the dress code regulations for women. According to official figures, four thousand men and women take part in the rally. Eyewitnesses speak of some five hundred demonstrators, many of whom are theology students.

In the weeks since I landed in Tehran, a lot has happened in Iran. European media, as usual, are concentrating on reports about nuclear energy disputes, the death penalty, and women's rights. They are all valid topics, and it is important to write about them, but it's not the whole picture. People who learn about the world from news programs tend to subconsciously categorize the images of extremes: the Africans starve, Afghanis carry out suicide bombings, Chinese plagiarize, and bearded Iranians tinker with their atom bomb. The daily grind is not mentioned, and even when everyday life is featured in reports about foreign lands, it is often in the form of romanticism— out with the modern and in with the traditional and old-fashioned. Who would present photos of shopping malls in Tehran or Shiraz that look almost exactly like their counterparts in Europe or North America? Readers and viewers easily forget that reality in every country is ten thousand times more diverse than what is shown.

A RIVER
WITHOUT WATER

IN THE LARGEST public square in the world that is completely enclosed by buildings and walls some urban sanitation workers are going through their morning exercises. They do aerobics to Eurodance music at club volumes. Somehow I had expected my first few minutes in Isfahan to be a more Oriental experience. The common name of the square is Naghsh-e Jahan, "Image of the World," so I suppose that turbaned water-pipe smokers or swirling dervishes also wouldn't really fit the bill. At precisely 5:45 AM the fountains are turned on, and forty-five minutes later the sun rises. Showtime.

At 1,800 feet by 500 feet, five times three soccer fields, it is framed by decorated two-tier arcades, mosque domes, palaces, and bazaar tunnels. It's impossible not to be overwhelmed by the dimensions. I arrived so early because the night bus from Hamedan took less than seven hours to get here. So as not to annoy my host with an early-morning alarm call, I have to putter around a bit.

One of the cheekier actions of the Ayatollah Khomeini was renaming Isfahan's architectural masterpiece "Imam Square." The word "imam" referred to himself, although he had absolutely nothing to do with it, as it was laid out over four hundred years ago by Shah Abbas. Before 1979 the official name was Shah Square for a couple decades. But most of the inhabitants couldn't care less about the ego trips of their leaders and still refer to the square as Naghsh-e Jahan.

Once again, I think it's a pity that there are no cafés here to while away some time, but in a side street I manage to find a tea house with wooden tables and men inhaling energy for the day through hookahs. About a third of the guests are bearded, turbaned men with long cloaks who mingle among the other guests giving advice from the *Quran* for their problems.

To: Sofia Isfahan
Good morning, I arrived in Isfahan now, how are you? Do you have time to meet today?

From: Sofia Isfahan
Hi, let's meet@ music school. I arranged a class for you. Don't hurry, but be there @ 10.30, not later

My host, Ahmad, lives twenty-five minutes by car north of the city center. Again, I call up a stranger, pass the phone to a cab driver, and gaze out of the window, curious about where he will drive me. Routine. A new day, a new apartment. Also routine. The excitement of always meeting new people is beginning to wear off.

Every long-term traveler knows the point when the usual "Where are you from/What's your name/Where did you go" conversations with other backpackers get on your nerves, even if you are talking to a potentially incredibly interesting person.

Ahmad greets me in jogging pants, a quiet but cheerful type who runs a T-shirt store in the city. Before my arrival I only had e-mail contact with Sofia, who arranged accommodation with Ahmad. It seems to be a common practice because Iranian women are afraid of breaking the rules and endangering their reputations by having male guests.

On the wall of Ahmad's bedroom there is a sheet with a handwritten saying on it. *Traveling is like flirting with life. It's like saying: You are beautiful and I love you, but I have to go.* A good idea: I have to go, too, and disappear with the next taxi. I contacted Sofia because she had written in her profile: *If u r interested in music and language u will have some good experience with me.* And because she's learning German. As I wrote that I was interested in Iranian instruments, she suggested showing me a music school and gave me the address for the cab driver.

At 10:27, three minutes too early, I'm standing in front of the door. Sofia is a wispy young lady dressed in a mustard-colored gown with an Indian-style pattern and ballerina shoes. The twenty-six-year-old manages to look both extravagant and traditional at the same time. Her eyes and lips are heavily made up but not overdone, like the fashionable young prefer it. I read in a survey that Iranian women buy more makeup than women in most other countries, and this can easily be ratified by a tour of any city here. The motivation to make the best out of that little bit of skin that is shown must be huge. Iran is also the world champion in the number of nose jobs performed.

Mr. Amini, the music theory teacher, leads us via a courtyard to the classrooms. We are allowed into various classrooms for a few minutes and listen to private concerts. Teenagers in black-and-white school uniforms beat with virtuoso precision on the tonbak, a goblet drum, and play the dulcimer-like santur, the kamancheh, a bowed string instrument, and the tar. The teacher hands me a tar, a wonderful instrument with the fingerboard made from camel bones; the body, in the shape of a figure 8, is carved from mulberry wood, with a thin membrane of lambskin stretched over the top. It is played with a small brass plectrum, with a grip for holding it made from beeswax, which sticks to the fingers. The tone is full, percussive, and sometimes jarring, similar to a clunking guitar. It is love at first sound, and I decide that I must get such an instrument.

"Where did you learn to play the tar?" asks Sofia, and suddenly I feel very Iranian.

"It's very similar to a guitar and so not too difficult for me."

She has an idea. "Would you like to do a guitar workshop with the children?"

"Sure!"

Mr. Amini agrees to do it the day after tomorrow, then we say goodbye and go on a short tour of the city. Isfahan is famous for its bridges over the Zayanderud, the "River of Life." At the moment, however, it's a dead river without a drop of water. A strip of desert that bisects the city. On the opposite bank there are a couple dozen pedal boats with swans necks as figureheads, high and dry on the riverbed.

"The government redirected the water, and nobody actually knows why. Maybe because fields had to be irrigated elsewhere. It hasn't rained much, and everything has just withered. We don't even know when we will have water here again," says Sofia. On a bank there is a No Swimming sign like a bad joke. Imagine Paris without the Seine or London without the Thames.

Green parks border on the river, and ancient grand stone bridges cross it. Now they are just decorations without practical use; you can just as easily walk to the other bank 15 or 150 feet either side of the bridges.

I ask Sofia if she's not annoyed that the water has been switched off.

"I don't think about the government," she says. "It's just a strain. Many people grumble the whole day. I simply get on with my life."

"And the moral police? Your shoes are pretty risky. I can see your ankle."

"Quite a lot of my outfit is risky—the makeup, even the color. But I work as an English teacher for girls of elementary school age, and the children love it when I wear colorful gowns. It's only the school directors who have problems with it."

She works at a private school, where only affluent parents can afford the afternoon classes, which cost 1 million toman a year ($400).

"I will ask if I can bring you as guest teacher."

From: Mona Hamedan
Ill miss you so much, you are really really kind & friendly, ich le be diech;-)

To: Mona Hamedan
I miss you too!! Too bad we had so little time in Hamedan!

204   We end our walk at Naghsh-e Jahan Square, where we meet André and Luciana from Brazil. They also contacted Sofia and, like me, were passed on to Ahmad. The two young doctors have a video camera, which they give me to film them doing a

three-second dance routine ending with them both screaming, "Elves in Isfahan!"

"We do a vlog where we present ourselves as elves on a trip around the world, and in every city we make such a clip," they explain. "And what do you do?"

"I'm working on a book, with pencil and notepad." I feel like a relic of bygone traveling days. All that is missing is telling them that I travel by coach and horses, pointing at one of the nearby carriages offering tours of the square.

It is getting dark, so we say goodbye to Sofia. Ahmad picks us up in his car and drives us to Khaju bridge, sandy yellow in the light of the night illuminations. "You're lucky I know a few secrets." He informs us that the bridge has thirty arches, fifteen on each side, and "that number corresponds to the Juz, or equal parts, of the Quran." Above each arch there are different floral designs made from decorative tiles. He then shows us what he calls the "oldest telephone in the world." At the end of the arches there are some tiny holes, and if you hold your ear to them you can clearly hear what someone has whispered into a hole diagonally opposite. Even the elves are impressed. We walk to a life-sized stone lion guarding the entrance to the bridge. In its jaws there is a human head. "That is a symbol for the power of the government over the people," says Ahmad quite matter-of-factly, as if it were a perfectly normal metaphor for the governors and the governed. "But now I'm going to tell you something really incredible! Have you seen a cat by night? How the eyes light up?" He points to an identical lion on the opposite bank of the dead river, three hundred feet away. Where its human head should be, two spots of light can be clearly seen. "You won't believe this but I once dreamed that the eyes glisten, and I came here and it really was just as

I had dreamed it." We can't explain the phenomenon; it must be some sort of reflection of the lamps at the entrance to the bridge.

Iran, spring 2014. A lion king with spotlight eyes eats human heads and guards the dried-up River of Life.

"Do you feel like some lamb's head?" asks Ahmad suddenly. "Or are you vegetarians?"

All three say no. So at this late hour we head for a corner restaurant in which a fat man with a bloody apron heaves braised lambs' heads from a huge cauldron with a kind of spade. This is served with a side plate of pita bread and a cloudy, fatty soup, on top of bits of brain, cheek, and jaw. Other pieces of offal appear on the table. "I always call the lungs 'hand towel,'" says Ahmad. "Because they have a surface just like terry cloth." They taste better than hand towels, but only just.

On the drive home he has one last highlight up his sleeve, just for me. Ahmad shows me a road sign with *Freiburg Avenue* on it. Quite a surprise, as I have become so used to all the Shariati-, Beheshti-, Azeri-, and Imam Khomeini streets, whose omnipresence is the cause of much confusion on street plans. "There is only one street with this name in Iran. Freiburg is twinned with Isfahan," Ahmad explains.

DICTATORSHIP

From: Sofia Isfahan
C u @ 10:00 music school:-)

· · · · · · · · · ·

THE FOLLOWING DAYS always begin with a text message containing brief instructions and a meeting place, followed by a colon, dash, and closed parenthesis. Orders and a smiley face—Sofia must be a good teacher. "I am the perfect dictator," she says when I bring up her nonconsultative style of planning the day.

The music teacher, Mr. Amini, has borrowed a guitar especially for me, a Yamaha, *Made in Indonesia*. The strings are so old that they have traces of rust in some places. We wait in a kind of reception room.

From nearby I hear the sound of applause, three times within a short interval. I ask myself what kind of activity has triggered that amount of enthusiasm. Then Mr. Amini rings the school bell; it is precisely 10:45. "Let's go!" he says, beckoning me to follow him.

We cross the courtyard and enter a hall. Some fifty schoolkids are sitting on yellow plastic chairs and are looking, full of expectation, toward the entrance. A single piano stool is on a raised stage with the obligatory Ayatollah Khomeini/Khamenei double portraits as a backdrop.

I walk toward the stage and again applause resounds; the previous times were just the trial runs. When I agreed to run a guitar workshop I had imagined two or three children asking me to show them the finger placement for G major or the chords to "Hotel California." Big mistake.

I sit down on the piano stool. Silence; expectant faces. A black hole forms in my stomach and tries to suck in the rest of my body, which would be a wonderful opportunity for me to disappear. I feel a strong pull, but unfortunately, I am not sucked away. Sophia sits at the back of the hall and positions her cell phone camera. Mr. Amini gives a short address and then, with a flourish of his hand, gestures to me. More applause. Never before have I been so frantically applauded just for showing up—maybe that is the best metaphor for Iranian hospitality.

"I will play two classical pieces by the Spanish composer Francisco Tárrega," I announce. I tune the guitar, giving me a few valuable seconds, and off I go with sweaty fingers. The piece is called "Lágrima," tears. Actually, I can play this piece in my sleep. I falter at two points, but nothing particularly bad. I continue with "Adelita," almost perfect, and now things are running smoothly, applause with stamping of the feet. The next song, "Someone Like You" by Adele, is a safe bet. Adele is popular everywhere in Iran. More applause.

Mr. Amini asks if anyone has any questions.

A small boy with horn-rimmed glasses sticks his hand up. "Can you play something heavier?"

The black hole reappears and sucks and sucks to no effect.

"If you can dance to it, then sure," says Mr. Amini, the skillful diplomat.

"Okay, I'll give it a go," I say. And so it comes to pass for the first time in the history of the music school an improvised rendition of Metallica's "Enter Sandman" is adapted for classical guitar. On average every fourth tone is wrong, but, to compensate, I am loud—and heavy. It's almost impossible to listen to it without moving to the beat. Fifty young boys in school uniform, however, manage without effort.

Restrained applause, and a few words of thanks from Mr. Amini. I have survived, and the children can go back to their classes.

"You were good," says Sofia.

Inside the magnificent throne room, murals depict fighting warriors on elephants, musicians strumming their instruments, and kings receiving other kings. We are sitting outside on the steps in front of the Chehel Sotoun pavilion, next to dumb-looking stone lion statues. To anyone eavesdropping, our conversation would sound a bit weird. "The tree is beautiful. The woman is pretty. The man is important," says Sofia in German. "I am not normal. The child is not exact. The tomato is free. I am free. We are free. The man is free. The woman is exact. That is positive."

"Where did you learn these funny sentences?" I ask.

"I copied them from an online language class." She had transcribed the words neatly into an exercise book and is now reading them out.

"I don't think it was a good web page. No one says, 'The woman is exact,'" I explain.

A European family with a small boy, probably about five, walk by. He is wearing huge sunglasses and a small baseball cap.

"Oh my God, is he cute!" squeals Sofia. "Do you think I could ask them if I can take a photo with him?"

She has already run to the bewildered parents and grabbed the child and given me her cell phone. I snap away as she kisses the boy on his cheeks. He seems a bit overwhelmed, since nobody asked him about this. Sofia gushingly thanks the parents.

"He wasn't that cute, a bit chubby," I say, trying to provide a slightly more objective viewpoint. But she is glowing, as if the tourist family had just told her she had won 10 billion rial in the lottery.

"Nonsense, he was awesome! Now I absolutely must go to Europe."

Mothers, hide your children.

"Are they all so cute there?"

"At least. You should have seen me at five."

"Sure! Come on, let's practice languages."

Not only Sofia's language skills but also my research project on love and marriage are making progress in Isfahan. For lunch I meet up with Massi, a very relaxed, pleasant soul with a black headscarf, who works as a broker at the stock exchange and occasionally as a tourist guide for official guests of the city. We go to a bistro in the Armenian quarter with waiters wearing black suspenders on white shirts. On the tables are tissue boxes from Hermès, and hanging from the ceiling are some mobiles, which on closer inspection turn out to be designer lamps, one consisting of dozens of yellow painted teapots, the other of knives and forks.

"Oh, so you're staying with Ahmad," says Massi. "He's crazy. I don't think anyone in Isfahan has as many guests." Massi is also very actively involved with couchsurfing and has organized many meetings. "Ahmad was arrested once because he was walking through the city with a foreign girl. The police threatened to withdraw the license for his shop, which is why he erased his profile. Now he only gets guests through friends."

"Have you ever had trouble with the police?" I ask.

"Not up to now, luckily. I don't think about it much. But some policemen showed an acquaintance of mine photos of one of our meetings in the park. That kind of thing is intimidating."

We are served Caesar salad and brightly colored smoothies. We could have been in any trendy neighborhood in any European city.

"I have a problem, and I would like to hear your opinion," says Massi suddenly.

"Sure, what is it?"

"I'm wondering if I should get married soon, I'm twenty-nine. I have gotten to know a nice man; he has a good job. He has just applied for a position with the State Department in Tehran."

"So, what's the problem?"

"He is quiet, and I'm an extrovert. We can't get along with each other so well. We're too different. He loves me, but I don't love him. At least not yet. I have no idea how I can make a decision. In Iran it's always the men who make the first move. Who knows if there'll be another opportunity."

"How long have you known each other?"

"We've met three times."

I almost choke on a salad leaf.

"And when did he propose?"

"Before the first date, on Facebook. We met at an official function and then became Facebook friends."

"Why are you in such a rush to get married?"

"When an Iranian woman lives alone, there's a lot of gossip and rumors. I'm getting pressure from my family. I shouldn't wait more than two years."

"But then you can take your time."

"Maybe he will lose interest."

"If he's serious about it, he can be patient for a couple months."

I find it difficult to give good advice because as far as the meaning and concept of marriage is concerned I come from a different planet.

In Iran the bride becomes all but the possession of the groom in marriage. As compensation he is required to finance the mutual apartment, and in the case of divorce he is obliged to pay a handsome divorce dowry. According to civil law, this is "the price for the woman for sleeping with the man during married life, for running the household and for obeying him."

Without his permission she cannot even leave the house, let alone the country.

According to the law, if a man wants a divorce, he just has to say, "I divorce you" three times to his wife. A woman with the same intention needs a court and her husband's signature. Subsequently, the man has the fundamental right to child custody. Prenup agreements that at least give some extra rights to women have become fashionable among young couples.

Anyway, remaining unmarried is not a solution, not only because of financial insecurity. The family and social pressures are strong, so very few women dare to stay single. Even those who are well educated and have top jobs, like Massi.

"You know that in Iran there are two weddings," she explains. "The first takes place within the inner circle, and afterward both partners still live with their families but start looking at apartments and furniture. In the process they get to know each other for the first time, since there are few opportunities otherwise. If you get divorced before the proper, big wedding ceremony, then it's not too dramatic. But it is still a divorce."

The male perspective on the subject is supplied by a chance encounter on the way back to Ahmad. I'm waiting on the roadside for a cab when a young man asks me if I want a lift. He is twenty-three, studies electronic technology, and introduces himself as Arash. "We are the lost generation," he says. "We have hardly any chance of a good job, and everything is getting more expensive. If I want to buy a house in a bad area, I have to work twenty years for it. For a house in a good area, one hundred years. To get married I have to own a bank."

All that is missing is a statement from Sofia. We meet up the next day in the park next to the Zayanderud riverbed. She

213

says that she doesn't understand how Europeans can have children without marrying. "The commitment is missing, isn't it? The man can do as he likes." If, however, you sign a contract and have a huge party with all your friends, then it is a real commitment. She has had a number of dates that were arranged by her parents. Her father is a very devout man who works as a tour guide for groups of pilgrims visiting sacred Shiite sites in Iraq. "Once there was a guy where absolutely nothing clicked. He just babbled such dumb stuff, I couldn't even look at him." Talking about the right age for having dates with the opposite sex, she thinks that kids younger than twenty should not get into it yet—it must be the teacher in her: "It distracts them from their schoolwork."

Once she almost stopped using the Couchsurfing portal because there was too much flirting. "At those meetings many people look for partners, and they try to persuade you to drink alcohol, put you under pressure, saying stuff like: 'Oh, so you're not a modern girl.' But, in effect, no girls are really modern. You just have to see them at home. The next problem is that many people want to be 'Western' when it's about parties and boys but not when it's about discipline and punctuality. They just cherry-pick."

DRUNK TO THE IMAM

ON THE HIGHWAY to the airport I feel pretty modern; I've just remembered that I still have a bottle of the best wine in western Iran in my backpack. Sofia's uncle Akbar is behind the wheel (actually, he's not her uncle, but in Iran a good friend from a generation above is often called "uncle"), next to him his wife, and behind her Sofia. He is an engineer and recently had a job offer from a telecommunication company called 3s Network in Irvine, California. In a few months he will emigrate to the U.S., and he's happy to be able to practice a bit of English with me.

On his cell phone he has stored 120 questions that he can expect to be asked at the interview for his visa application in Tehran—and the answers. He knows almost all of them by heart, as shown by the following role-play in which I become the stern consulate official.

"Who interviewed you for the job, and how many interviews did you have?"

"I had three phone interviews with Mr. Hawkins."

"How did you hear about the company?"

"The CEO is from Iran; he is a friend of my brother-in-law."

"How do you know the company is real?"

"I talked to some employees, and I checked the website."

"Why will you come back to Iran?"

"Because of my family."

"Why do you want to change?"

"I will earn more money and learn more in my field."

He explains that in Iran you won't get rich from engineering. "Here I earn $350 a month, and in the U.S. more like $5,000." He really wants to make it happen. Only a year ago he could say little more than "Hello" and "How are you?" Now he does nothing other than practice English with his private tutor. I wish him luck when I say my goodbyes.

"Pray for me at the shrine of Imam Reza in Mashhad," says Sofia and shakes my hand. "Tell him that I want to go to Germany, and that he should make it happen."

"Will do. You are the best dictator in this country," I say.

I have an hour to wait before my flight to one of Islam's most sacred cities. The wine has to go. In my mind I beg forgiveness from His Majesty Ehsan, prince and master winemaker of Marivan. There are a thousand better places to relish the pleasures of a fruity 2013 vintage than the toilets of the Shahid Beheshti Airport in Isfahan. In two minutes I manage two thirds of the bottle; the rest I tip into the bowl. A mighty fine wine. I have to flush twice until there's no more evidence of red. Now I just have to dispose of the bottle, pop some chewing gum into my mouth, and voila. I walk as straight as possible to the counter, and my drunken mind realizes that you just need to swap two letters to turn "check in" into "chicken." I show my ticket and wait in line for the security controls.

216

From: Sofia Isfahan
Sorry I couldn't have even a small hug with u @ airport in
front of my friends U know maybe they find it strange;-)
Was nice meeting u. U r so kind:)

To: Elaheh Mashhad
Hi elaheh, i m on my way now, i will arrive at the airport in
around 3 hours. see you soon!

From: Elaheh Mashhad
My address is manouchehri st. call me when you get to the
cab.

From: Massi Isfahan
Have a great rest of trip. please pray for me at imam reza
shrine!:)

An announcement crackles through the loudspeakers: "Mister Stephan, please come to the information desk." I'm not
sure whether I heard the name correctly. Have I lost something? Passport and ticket are in my hands, so I don't think so.
Did the security cameras film me disposing of the bottle, and
they have found traces of wine in the garbage? I decide not to
go to the information desk. In the waiting room at the gate
the announcement is repeated, but again it's not really under-
standable. They must mean someone else. The wine is making
me confused.

I try to be rational and to channel all my anxieties toward
the approaching flight. I booked with Taban Air, a tiny company with seven planes. The maintenance problems in Iran's
air-traffic trade are well known. Imported spare parts are scarce,

217

certainly for the American MD-88 plane onto which I am about to board. The country's aircraft mechanics are the jazz musicians of engineers. Masters of improvisation, who also sometimes integrate unusual tones and waive conventional solutions. I deliberate about whether on my plane the onboard electronics, the hydraulics, or the engines are most likely to be cobbled together with parts from the Saipa automobile plant. Or all three. Whether some technicians, like musicians, are better at improvising than others after drinking a couple glasses of wine. It'll fly all right, won't it? *Inshallah.* I google Taban Air's last crash landing. It was four years ago. Coincidentally, it was the Isfahan to Mashhad route, forty-two injured. Four years could mean one of three things:

a) As a reaction to the incident security has been improved considerably.

b) It's about time it happened again.

c) I'm worrying too much.

The correct answer proves to be c. The pilot takes off elegantly, stays up in the air the intended amount of time, and lands as gently as a feather of a mynah bird on a Persian carpet.

RELIGION AND MONEY

"**H**AVE YOU GOT swimming gear with you? This afternoon there is a pool party," says Elaheh. That isn't the kind of sentence I expected to hear in strictly religious Mashhad. But actually I should have realized by now that Iran takes great pleasure in twisting expectations, crumpling them up, and then with great panache, dumping them in a huge garbage can marked: *Prejudices, Official Perceptions, and Theocracy.* So, to the holy shrine in the morning and to a party in the afternoon— the agenda appeals to me.

Elaheh is a dentist, and she looks a little like former world number one tennis pro Ana Ivanovic and has a friend named Ismail, who picks us up in an ancient Jeep without a windshield. To cruise around the holy city in this vehicle is pure pleasure—at last, the feeling of freedom outside walls and fences. With airflow in your face and the sun in your hair you begin wondering why on Earth cars are built with windshields. Mashhad is a rich city and seems to be more modern and cleaner than Tehran or Isfahan. Every year more than 15 million pilgrims come here. At the roadside there are huge billboards advertising real estate, and the pedestrian bridges seem to be brand new. Huge construction cranes numbered 1 to 9 herald the building of the largest shopping center in the country. At a subway station we change to a more modern form of transport, with more windows than we've become used to, and travel to the center.

Fifteen million pilgrims. Imagine a sold-out AT&T Stadium, more than 80,000 people. Now imagine ten or twenty AT&T stadiums, and you are not even close. Every year the number of Muslims arriving would fill 190 full AT&T stadiums. Some official sources speak of 20 million—250 football stadiums. But you should be a little careful with such figures. Maybe the state propaganda machinery would like to make the Iranians a bit more devout than they really are.

Imam Reza didn't cause much of a stir during his lifetime 1,200 years ago. But he is the eighth of twelve imams, so for Shiites a legitimate heir of Mohammad and thus worthy of honor. They also believe that he was done away with by Caliph Harun al-Rashid using poisoned grapes (historians are less certain), which would allow him the status of martyr. The other ten imams (they are still waiting for the return of the twelfth imam, for whom there is no grave) were buried outside Iran. The mausoleum isn't a cemetery but a palace. The whole complex, consisting of almost 20 million square feet, is, in terms of area, the largest mosque in the world, and one third larger than the equivalents in Mecca and Karbala.

220

We meet up with the architect Parisa, a friend of Elaheh and Ismail, and I'm left alone with her, as they are not interested in shrines. They take my camera, as I'm not allowed in with it, although, funnily enough, it's okay to take pictures with a cell phone.

The next two hours Parisa and I spend walking from one huge courtyard to the next, passing mighty vaulted iwans and gilded entrances. Uniformed officials with color-coded dusters in their hands maintain order.

"Yellow stands for a guide specializing in general questions, green for religious ones," explains Parisa. The guides are allowed to poke women (and men) with their dusters who go the wrong way. In many areas and entrances there are strict rules about gender segregation. There is supposed to be a waiting list of ten thousand men wanting to work here, which probably has more to do with the proximity to the holy shrine than the opportunity to poke people.

Time and again Parisa is warned by the watchdogs to completely cover her hair and fingernails, painted in mosque dome turquoise. In the whole shrine chadors are obligatory for women. The splendor of the gigantic complex is overwhelming. "I once showed a French tourist around, and he thought that the Palace of Versailles suddenly seemed small and modest," says Parisa. The holy shrine is constantly being extended, for more than a thousand years already. In the meantime space has become scarce, forcing them to build underground praying areas whose access staircases resemble those of a subway station. They lead to mirrored halls with hundreds of prayer rugs and hundreds of chandeliers.

The chandeliers all have white bulbs except for one that is green. "That one is to mark the nearest to the grave," says Parisa. Masses of pilgrims jostle toward a kind of golden cage behind which Reza's sarcophagus is concealed. As a non-Muslim I am not permitted to go as far as the cage. Also, emotionally I would stick out—most of the visitors are praying and many are crying for the martyr. I am just stunned. In my mind I ask Imam Reza for an early trip to Germany for Sofia, for a decent husband for Massi, and for an extension to my visa, which is due in five days.

You don't dare to think what such buildings must have cost. A business conglomerate consisting of mining concerns, a bus factory, textile companies, agricultural businesses, and a large proportion of the land on which the city stands funds the Imam Reza Shrine. The hotels accommodating the pilgrims have to pay a levy for the land. Such businesses are called bonyads and as official charitable trusts are exempt from tax and take donations. They are under the control of the Supreme Leader Khamenei, who was born in Mashhad. There are 120 bonyads in Iran, and they are a considerable economic factor. The largest of them runs the Imam Reza Shrine and has an annual turnover of US$14 billion; that's more than Porsche.

PARTY

ISMAIL DOESN'T HAVE a Porsche, but his old Jeep is just as much fun. In the afternoon we drive a short distance out north of the city. Our driver stops at a heavy iron gate that looks as if you would have to punch in a password and convince a boxing champion's minder of your good intentions, but in fact, it swings gently open to let us in. We park behind two other cars on a gravel path; trance music warbles from a Peugeot.

"Have you got any weed?" asks a man who looks nothing like a Persian boxing champion but like a heavily tattooed gangsta rapper. In fact, he is a filmmaker.

"Sorry," answers Ismail.

"Something to drink?"

"Also no."

Mina, a friend of Elaheh, is already there, as well as three men. The party location is in a garden behind a fifteen-foot-high wall concealing all from prying eyes. An acidic fruit called "green tomatoes" and mulberries grow here, and directly next to the entrance there is a swimming pool some 30 feet long and 6.5 feet deep. In a small outhouse with a kitchen and living room we change, one after the other. Soon, two women in bikinis and five men in shorts are hopping into the ice-cold water. Ismail uses a GoPro camera with a watertight case and film, especially when the women are swimming. In particular the well-built Mina seems to relish the interest that her body arouses. I am astonished by her trust in Ismail not to do something stupid with the film, like posting it on Facebook. I feel like a reporter who has been invited to a secret porn shooting location. The difference is that being caught at a porn shoot in Europe would cause you considerably less trouble.

With my expensive camera I am also asked to snap a few photos. Men on the seats of the Jeep, women on the hood. Sensational material that would send the moral police into frenzies. Unfortunately, I will never be able to publish them.

"There's nothing to drink, so what shall we do?" Elaheh asks the mother of all questions. We sit around on plastic chairs and eat melon and smoke miniature cigarettes called Bahman. I learn how to say "Your father is a dog" and "Eat shit" in Persian and in return teach the others a few filthy German phrases. Just because this party is forbidden doesn't automatically mean that it's a good one.

On the way back in the late afternoon we stop at the Venice Café, which is as close to a cozy European pub as you can get without selling alcohol. Behind the bar there are rows of bottles containing different colored liquids, not spirits but fruit syrups. The words La fortuna può grande è trovare felicità nelle piccole cose—Happiness is enjoying the small things in life—are written in white chalk on a board. How true. At the moment I'm enjoying the aroma of a real cappuccino; at last, a coffee that's not based on the ubiquitous Nescafé. The interior with wooden walls is so dark that the faces of the young guests are mainly illuminated by their tablets or cell phones, on which they play *Castle Clash* or send a few words and loads of emoticons via Viber. Viber and Telegram are the most popular communication apps because WhatsApp doesn't always work here.

There are also pauses in our communications because we are distracted by the glare of the screens. Elaheh orders a French coffee and talks of illegal drugs. "I think, in fact, the government has nothing against them because they stop people from getting silly ideas. If you are high you don't start a revolution." She inhales her Bahman cigarette with obvious pleasure. "Apart from that, it's written in the *Quran* that alcohol is forbidden, but there are no clear instructions about hash, opium, or heroin."

"Aren't you frightened of getting caught drinking?"

"It's a game of chance; up to now I've been lucky."

We again turn back to our cell phones. Elaheh studied dentistry for five years in Istanbul, was in Europe three times, knows Hamburg, Berlin, and Münster. Her father is a banker, her mother is a biologist, and they share an apartment. In Europe she would be considered to have high potential. In Mashhad, the second-largest city in Iran, she can't find a job. "At the moment I'm assisting a bit in a dental practice just for the experience; I don't earn anything."

Elaheh has two siblings, a brother who is an engineer and a sister who is a doctor. Both moved away long ago and now live in the U.S. Probably she will soon follow them abroad. Like so many people who are highly educated she has no prospects in her home country, and on top of that, she has had bad experiences with Iranian men. "Most of them are

225

interested in only two things: money and pornography," says Elaheh.

A friend of hers joins us—who is as plump as he is chirpy—businessman Mehdi, who deals in electronic parts and fittings. He speaks perfect English, because he lived for a number of years in Toronto, and talks nineteen to the dozen. He tells us about an Arabian prince who bought golden light switches from him, about the Italian ambassador in Tehran who is much more relaxed than his stuffy German equivalent, about a crash landing a few days ago in the eastern Iranian city of Zahedan and the friend who survived it, about the electronic trade fair in Frankfurt that he visited in March. And about Mashhad.

"My friends in Tehran think that Mashhad is boring because of all the religious fanatics, but it's not true. There is everything here that you could want: parties, good cafés, everything. As long as you avoid Haram, the area where the shrine is, you can live well here."

Mehdi is not interested in religious destinations; for him there are far more interesting alternatives. "From time to time I make a pilgrimage to Amsterdam. Last year I took a couple magic mushrooms and went to the flower show at Keukenhof—that was incredible. For two days I only wandered around with sunglasses." Enlightenment for all: Muslims make pilgrimages to the shrine in Mashhad and nonreligious Mash-hadis make pilgrimages to Dutch coffee shops.

LOST IN
VISA APPLICATION

I'M NOT SURE whether Imam Reza heard my request for a visa extension. The necessary stamp didn't materialize in my passport overnight, so the next morning I take a cab to the Foreign Affairs Office to be grilled in a plain waiting room by a small man in a fine gray suit.

"Why do you want to extend your stay here?" he asks, his tone implying that I had asked him whether he needed a naked cleaner for his apartment.

"I love traveling in Iran; I like it very much here." One of the few sentences in the ensuing hours that is the complete truth.

"What are you doing in Mashhad?" he demands.

"Visiting the holy shrine."

"Where did you get the first extension?"

"In Kerman."

"What did you do there?"

"I made a tour of the Kaluts in the desert. I'm interested in the whole country; I want to see as much of Iran as possible," I say, trying to win him over.

"Then you should do it in twenty days." He stabs the date in my original visa with his index finger to emphasize his point.

"So I can't extend it here?"

"Go to the police station, Imam Reza Street 1, and ask there."

He turns away. He seems to have decided that our conversation is over. I take a cab to Imam Reza Street.

The cab driver must have misunderstood me. He lets me out at a tiny police post at a roundabout, where two weary policemen are keeping watch. There's no way that they will have a visa extension stamp in the drawer of their desk, is there? Well at least it's the right street. I suppose I could ask them where the main police station is, but it all seems a bit odd. If you can't renew a visa in the Foreign Affairs Office, how on Earth would it be possible here? And isn't a voluntary visit to the Iranian police something that a multiple lawbreaker simply has to avoid?

I walk down a street that consists almost solely of hotels and souvenir stores. Studio photos of kids grotesquely spruced up, using Photoshop to embed them in front of the Reza shrine dome, seem to be very popular.

On a corner I see the *Aria Travel Agency* sign and buy a bus ticket for the next day to a town on the Caspian Sea. Then I ask about the prospects of getting a visa extension. The boss himself offers his help and grabs the telephone to make inquiries.

228   "Impossible," he then says.

"Impossible? In Mashhad or in all of Iran?"

"In the whole country. But you could go to another office and talk to the people there."

"Do you think it's worth it?"

"If you ask me, no chance. Big problem."

"And at the police station?"

"No, they can't speak English. I'll write down the address of another visa office."

"And they will understand me?"

"Yes, but it's still absolutely inconceivable that you will get an extension to your visa."

Back on the street I hold the paper with the address under a cab driver's nose. After twenty minutes he stops outside a green wall in a side street off Piruzi Boulevard. "*Edareh-ye Gozarnameh*," he says, the name of the office that the man in the travel agency gave me. A narrow entrance leads to a courtyard with wood-paneled reception huts, and a couple armed soldiers walk around busily. The counter clerk greets me with a radiant smile.

"Hello, where do you come from?" he asks.

"Germany."

"Ooh, Germany! Welcome to Mashhad! You probably want your visa extended. Please go into the main building, turn left, and speak to my friend!" I am so surprised by the friendly reception that I almost drop my passport.

The "friend" in the next room carries on where the other left off.

"How are you?"

"Fine, thanks."

What can I do for you?"

"I'd like to extend my visa."

"Okay, fill out this form. How long is your visa valid?"

"Another five days."

"Okay."

"How long will the formalities take?"

"Roughly five days."

"Oh, I'm traveling on tomorrow. Is there not a possibility of speeding things up?"

"Maybe. Maybe not."

The warmth of the official is in stark contrast to the austere waiting room ambience of his office. *Please don't ask unnecessary questions to save the time of the staff and other customers* is written on a poster. Another shows a portrait of Ayatollah Khamenei with the words: *If the leader order, we attack. If want our head, we grant our head.* A third poster is all about information for foreigners wanting to marry Iranian women: *Please respect the valid laws, otherwise expect prison sentences from one to three years.*

I fill out the form. German address, name of father, reason for travel (tourism), profession (website editor), Hotel (Al-Naby. It was the first hotel listed in *Lonely Planet*). I give the piece of paper to a third official in a neighboring room, where a glass pane, with a tiny slit to pass the forms through, separates the applicant from the clerks. Above it there is an LED display with the calling numbers .167. 199. 267. A loud *ping* accompanies each new illuminated number.

"Is it possible to have it dealt with today?" I ask.

"I will check." Two minutes later: "It could be possible, particularly as you are German. We like the Germans." A slim man in military uniform, he glances at my application. "What a coincidence; I'm also a website editor. Which programming language do you use?"

"I write the content; I don't program." Now it's getting tricky.

"Who do you work for?"

"I'm freelance and do advertising. For museums and cultural institutions." He seems satisfied.

"Are you single?" is his next question.

"Yes," I answer, too nervous about my Münchhausen job description to find the question adequately disconcerting.

"Excuse me, this isn't an official question, but how tall are you?"

"6" 2'."

"Exactly as tall as me! We have a lot in common! How much do you earn a month?" So much for *Please avoid unnecessary questions.*

A fourth official joins us. Obviously, I'm the high point of an otherwise uneventful day.

"Hamburg! Mahdavikia!" he says.

"Ali Daei! Ali Karimi!" I respond. Party mood at the visa office. If it goes on like this, we will all become Facebook friends and meet up later for a couple beers. But back to business. A colleague returns with my application. "We have to translate it into Persian. Could you fill in the hotel address." I copy the address from the guidebook in capital letters. Molla Hashem Lane, not far from the shrine. Imam Reza, *please* extend my visa. "Take a seat. You will be called."

A number of different things go through your head while waiting in an Iranian government agency after having told a

231

few half-truths. Hopefully they don't call my phony hotel. Why didn't I just say I was a student instead of a website editor, like Yasmin did at the police station in Kurdistan? What do I tell them if they google my name and discover that I work for a large news site and not for a little museum? So many questions. At least one of the other posters gives me some hope: *Patience is the key to success and prosperity comes to those who wait.*

Time and again I hear the thump of stamps, but none of them on my passport.

"Mr. Stephan," is suddenly announced. I go to the counter, to an official I haven't yet seen. The bucket seat is fixed at ninety degrees to the window so that it isn't too comfortable.

The man looks at me with a serious face and says: "Hmm." Pause. My passport is in his right hand. "We have a problem," he continues.

Stay cool, don't forget to breathe, look unsuspicious. "What kind of problem?" I ask.

"You were in Kerman and extended your visa there. We have to investigate that more thoroughly. You can come again on Wednesday." That is in three days.

"But I have a bus ticket for tomorrow."

"Hmm. Take a seat."

Patience is the key to success. Patience is the key to success. Patience. In *Lonely Planet* I read: "Mashhad is not the best place to extend visas." I sit there for 1 hour, 1.5 hours.

Thumping stamps, blinking three-digit numbers, groggy brain. *Ping,* 188. If the leader orders, we attack. *Ping,* 211. Mahda-vikia. *Ping,* 286. Are you single? *Ping,* 189. We like Germans. *Ping,* 212. In Kerman they smoke opium so that plane passengers in the air overhead can get high. *Ping,* 190. Patience is the key to success.

"Mr. Stephan!" I almost miss hearing my name. I go to the counter. The 6"2' website editor passes me my passport—with a stamp valid until May 28, 2014, four extra weeks. "Please sign here. Goodbye!"

GREEN, WHITE, RED

THE **LONG-DISTANCE BUS** edges through the traffic jam on the outskirts of the city, where hundreds of Iranian flags and green, white, and red lights decorate the fringe of the highway. Three colors: green for belief, red for the blood of martyrs, and wedged in between, white for peace and friendship. A sword emblem with four crescent moons, stylized representations of the name of God, are emblazoned on the white background, as if to show that, when in doubt, weapons and Allah are more important than peace. But what kind of country is it really, over which this flag flies?

For me it is a country that enchants and enrages me at the same time. It enchants because there are such magical places, like Yazd, Shiraz, or Isfahan, and the countryside is magnificent, and because the warmth of the people is unique in the world. It enrages me because a state religion is imposed on the people without giving them a free choice. Because there are not enough opportunities for the young to make something of their lives. Because it is a rich country with gigantic oil and gas reserves, but most people have not benefited from them. They are like Cassim in the cave of treasures in *Ali Baba and the Forty Thieves*, surrounded by riches but trapped.

In Mashhad I experienced the contrast between the two Irans, the two realities that coexist side by side, particularly strongly. On the one hand, the theocracy, where people mourn their martyr at the golden cage in the imam mausoleum. And on the other, a "hide-and-seek-ocracy," where people hold secret parties and seek worldly thrills instead of spiritual bliss.

I have visited numerous countries on all continents and nowhere have I experienced a stronger difference between public show and private reality.

And nowhere have I experienced such a pronounced culture of making do—they navigate as expertly around the laws as an Iranian driver through traffic jams.

Satellite dishes are forbidden, but in some neighborhoods you see them attached to every house. Tight women's clothing and headscarves perched high on the head are against regulations, but in the afternoons in parks of Tehran or Shiraz they are omnipresent. Facebook is forbidden, but every person under forty uses it. And increasingly, older people, too, even Ayatollah Khamenei and President Rouhani. Both are also active on Twitter, which is blocked in Iran.

Outside it is night. Every now and then we pass the lights of towns and villages—Qushan, Shirvan, Gorgan. Patriotic monuments on roundabouts, martyr paintings on concrete walls, portraits of the bearded leaders. Every town is plastered with propaganda from the Islamic Republic. How many people living behind windows secretly long for a different regime? How many are happy with life in the only Shiite nation in the world? And how many are living in fear of their own government?

235

The bus conductor, a man around fifty, with a mustache and baggy jeans, asks to see my ticket. I pass it to him. He points to my Adidas sunglasses. "How much?" he wants to know. Unasked, he then explains the difficulties of being a Muslim. "No whiskey, no beer, no *digi digi*." What he means by the latter he shows me by pushing his right index finger in and out of the ring made from his left index finger and thumb. "Go Thailand, China—*digi digi* no problem for Muslim." Again the gesture, then he moves on to the next passenger.

People who think Iran is a country of prudes are wrong. In religious programs on TV they go into great detail about the torment of male abstinence. Men are seen as wild beasts who can hardly control their sexual energies. An extremely comfortable perspective for those with the Y chromosome because then it is up to the women not to provoke them. If they do so, then they have to face the consequences. The obvious question of why such easily corruptible beasts have the last word in all matters is not asked in the Islamic Republic.

At the moment, a video clip from a popular TV talk show is a hit (also among the younger generation, who think of it as a curiosity and pass it around on their cell phones). In the clip Ayatollah Khamenei demands Iranians procreate. "Every couple should have five children, even better eight or fourteen," says the supreme leader, sitting in front of an image of a mosque. "Start today! Say 'Ya Ali' and 'Ya Zahra' and get going! "Ya Ali"—"In the name of Ali"—is a phrase that is often used before performing difficult tasks or unpleasant duties. Imagine the U.S. president giving such a pep talk to the nation on the *Ellen DeGeneres Show*.

236

The film on the onboard TV is somewhat more innocent. It is about a rich guy who falls in love with a poor thief. The family is against the match, but with a bit of shrewdness and some histrionics she is eventually able to win over everybody and outmaneuver her wealthy but boring rival. "Iranian films always have a happy ending," an acquaintance from Tehran once told me. "Because the reality is already bad enough."

FUN

THE MOST BRAZEN character I meet in all my travels in Iran is fifty-three, has a mustache and a khaki vest, and is named Mohamed. His nickname, with which he signs off his e-mails, suits him far better: "Funman." We meet in front of an ice cream parlor in Abbas Abad, a small town on the Caspian Sea, which consists mostly of a main street and the rows of houses bordering it.

"I love ice cream," announces Funman. He shouts the words; his vocal chords don't seem to be designed for quieter tones. "Why are so many people unhappy or stressed? One ice cream is enough to be happy," he bellows while bearing two full cones from the counter. "And that is the most important thing in life—to have fun!" We have known each other all of a minute, but already there is a motto for the next couple days.

"Tonight I have been invited to a wedding. My son is not here, so will you come instead?" He scrutinizes me from head to foot. After being on the road for more than six weeks I am a suitable candidate for detergent ads—for the "before" pictures. "Have you got anything suitable to wear?" he asks.

Funman has a white Honda 125 motorbike, with tin panniers on which he has written his phone number and e-mail address. A sociable man. He has attached an adventurous construction on top of the speedometer, consisting of tape, twine, a JVC car radio, and a loudspeaker with an eight-inch diameter. "I've traveled a lot with this," shouts Funman. "I used to be a truck driver. In my whole life I haven't spent more than ninety days at home. Come on, my store isn't far away, just down the road to the umbrella." I walk ahead; he drives.

The store is a small snack bar, with plastic tables and maps all over the walls. Funman's wife, Mahboube, is cooking ash soup that she serves in plastic bowls. "I will introduce you to a couple friends at the wedding. And you will meet many beautiful girls. It starts at nine!" screams Funman.

"No, my dear, at eight," corrects Mahboube in a soft voice. She is very conservatively dressed and radiates serenity—they couldn't be more different.

I give them a pack of walnut cookies as a present. My marzipan reserves have long been exhausted.

"I looove cookies, how did you know that? Thanks! I won't give one of them away!" is the reaction of the patriarch. Carrying on, word for word: "Do you want the Internet? Come on, let's be Facebook friends! I need music! My wife thinks I'm too loud. Aaaah, cyclists!" He dashes out to the main road, where a couple mountain bikers *whoosh* past. My host has the composure of a swarm of wasps whose nest was just hit by a rock.   239

"I *love* cyclists," he explains on returning. "I'm registered on Warm Showers, which is a platform only for cyclists looking for accommodation." All in all he has provided accommodation for three hundred to four hundred visitors in the last 2.5 years. Funman picks up a foot-long toy Porsche that was lying next to a computer on a desk and turns a knob. "Brother Louie" by Modern Talking blares out; the toy car has an embedded MP3 player. Déjà vu: the worst song of the 1980s had already irritated me in Kurdistan and now it's followed me to the Caspian Sea.

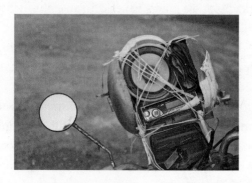

With these sonic waves, Funman, now apparently at peace finally, can devote himself to work and begins tapping away at his computer. Mahboube serves up a delicious soup, and then I rummage around in my backpack for my black shirt. I eventually discover it; it's still clean and unused.

"Haven't you got one in a more cheerful color?" asks Funman. He turns out the light in the store, turning up the racing-car stereo unit now playing "Happy Nation" by Ace of Base. He then stands up and dances around in the dark for a few seconds.

· · · · · · · · · ·

THE WEDDING RECEPTION at the Vazik Hotel is in full swing, with a couple hundred guests in suits and evening dresses— and one visitor in jeans and a black shirt. In the car park there is a shiny white Hyundai with a floral decoration on its hood. A kind of pavilion leads to a dining area and to an octagonal room with a dance floor. Most of the women aren't wearing veils but risqué short skirts and high heels beyond the four-inch mark. Naturally, it's against the rules, but the happy couple would have taken precautions. A handsome bundle of bank notes deposited at the local police station will ensure that no one mistakenly patrols the Vazik this evening.

A group of men sitting at a wooden table on the other side of the car park also benefit from this. Funman takes me there and introduces me to some of his friends. A young man with a neat haircut and a particularly fine suit pours out raisin schnapps, which is only drinkable once Delster lemon-flavored nonalcoholic beer is added.

Group photos are taken. Only the young man with the bottle doesn't want his picture taken. "He's in the navy," explains Funman. He is afraid because a photo of him at a booze-up posted on Facebook or Instagram could get him into trouble. Another man approaches me with glassy eyes and kisses me three times on the cheeks.

"I always wanted to kiss a German," he slurs and raises his arm in a Hitler salute with so much swing that he almost loses balance. "But I'm not gay!"

A friend pushes him aside. "Don't worry about him, he's crazy."

The drinks are strong enough to knock out a horse and of a dubious quality, and I'm glad to hit the dance floor after three schnapps. "Let's see how the younger generation reacts to you," says Funman.

At first they don't react at all. But I'm quite content simply to observe the happenings from a chair draped in silk. The

241

newlyweds dance a waltz alone. The groom is about three heads taller than the bride. She appears to be a bit tense and sweats profusely in her multilayered wedding dress. The DJ, who is standing directly behind me, has bodybuilder biceps and is continuously shouting something into the microphone. The stereo system is turned up louder than in most German clubs, and Funman stands directly in front of the speaker. "I looove loud music," he screams. "Come on, get on the dance floor!"

I obey, if only to move away from the speaker. Persians are excellent dancers—with abandon they swirl over the parquet floor, gleaming faces everywhere, a wonderful party. Most have more grace in their little fingers than I have in my whole body. Stylistically, the greatest difference is in the arm movements. Iranians seldom have their elbows below their shoulders, whereas Europeans tend to keep their arms nearer their bodies. In direct comparison it looks like a chicken attempting to fly. "You don't dance particularly well," says Funman, as I sit back down after five songs.

Still, the evening brings one historic moment of joy: a girl named Setareh mistakes me for Funman's son and only later realizes that I am a foreigner. She thought I was Iranian! Mission accomplished; I've made it! I step forward in front of the whole gathering, appeal for silence with a casual wave at the DJ, wait a couple seconds for the suspense to rise and then, grabbing the mike, announce Kennedy-like, "*Ich bin ein Iraner.*" No, of course I don't do that, it was just a fantasy induced by raisin schnapps. But it would have been great fun.

ORWELL

MY ACCOMMODATION IS a villa with a large garden for me alone. Twenty years ago it must have been beautiful; now it just has a certain charm.

"Are you afraid of the dark?" asks Funman on opening the iron gate to the jungle of a garden. The front door opens directly to the kitchen, and we are hit by an appalling stench. Funman swears. "That was the Australians. They were the last ones here. Why don't they just think a bit before leaving the remains of their kebabs? That's one of the reasons that my wife doesn't like couchsurfing." The living room and bedroom smell a bit better—the first of builder's rubble and the second of damp bedspreads. Nothing has been cleaned or tidied here for months. As usual there is no bed, so I make myself comfortable on the carpet. A few dogs bark outside. "Here is the stereo unit. You can hook it up to your cell phone," says Funman before disappearing into the dark.

Floorboards creak in the night, outside an animal rustles about, and I think I hear the sound of footsteps. The biggest shock, however, comes in the morning, with the sound of a rattling motorbike to the accompaniment of music blasting through the garden. The machine falls silent, and now the Latino pop tearjerker can be recognized: "Could I Have This Kiss Forever" by Enrique Iglesias.

"Stephan! Are you awake?" screams a hoarse but familiar voice. Unnecessary question, as that entrance would have woken the dead. "I want to show you a few things here in town. You'll definitely like them!"

A short time later a drowsy tourist and a hyperactive fun man enter the library of Abbas Abad. To the left a staircase leads to the reading room for women; men have to use the right-hand one. A woman in a black chador sits in the middle of the room, behind her are rows and rows of books, and Ayatollah Khamenei can be seen on a poster reading the *Quran*.

"Go and ask her something. Let's see how she reacts," insists Funman, the amateur sociologist.

So I go up to her and ask her something: "Do you have any books in English?"

She appears uneasy, looks at Funman, and speaks to him in Persian. He indicates that she should address me directly. "Yes," she says and then, "Come." She leads me to a shelf and then dashes back to reception. In addition to a couple dictionaries and software manuals, there is one single novel: George Orwell's *Animal Farm*. According to the stamp, the book has only been borrowed twice, which is a pity, as it is a fantastic read. The story describes an animal revolt on a farm, resulting in the new regime proving to be worse than the previous one. *Oh Allah, save me from the darkness of ignorance* is written on a poster on the wall.

"Where are you from?" asks the librarian. Suddenly, she feels a bit more confident about chatting. Her English is good, but she seems to have had more practice at reading than talking. Her name is Fatimeh, and her husband writes poetry. She has a master's in biology and originally comes from Tehran. But to her the north is much more beautiful—better air and greener.

In the meantime, Funman has made friends with a cleric in a turban and a long kaftan. In the computer corner he is showing him photos from his couchsurfing profile. For instance, the photo of him enjoying an Efes beer in Turkey.

The cleric winces slightly, and then quickly regains his composure. "He's a relaxed man. He knows that people drink alcohol; he just doesn't do it himself," explains Funman. "Good guy. There are good people everywhere, even a few with turbans. He was a preacher at the Friday mosque for years. Go on, ask him something!"

This little outing with Funman isn't proving to be particularly relaxing. "Err... how important is religion in your everyday life?" I manage to ask hesitantly. I can't think of anything cleverer to say without getting too political.

"I pray no more than other people," says the good cleric, adding that he regrets not being able to speak English. "The *Quran*

245

schools have only recently begun to offer English classes." He then says goodbye, as he has to go to the mosque.

"*Berim*," says Funman, too—let's go. I also say "*berim*" to practice my Persian, and he laughs.

"Not like that. You have to roll the 'r.'"

"I can't"

"It's simple: *rrrrr!*"

"I can't do it. We don't have that kind of 'r' in German, at least not where I come from."

"Nonsense, everyone can do it."

"Okay, say 'Eichhörnchen.'"

"*Eickhern-Ken!*"

"No, *Eichhörnchen*. It's easy."

"*Ai-Kern-Shen!*"

"Totally wrong. Let's go. *Berim!*"

"*Ei-Shern-Ken!*"

We both laugh, and then go for an ice cream.

"Did you notice how shy the girl in the library was?" asks Funman while playing with his scoop of chocolate ice cream. "It's pathetic! We teach the young to be afraid. We don't think them capable of anything, we pamper them, never allow them to jump in the deep end."

"Actually, she could speak quite good English."

"If you live within a system of fear, it rubs off on you. It is not only the government that keeps this system alive but also the parents who restrain their children out of fear."

"Why don't you go away?"

"I love my country. If the government were to give us just a little more freedom, not as many people would leave. Today it is hot, so I would love to go out in my shorts. I'm not allowed. We have beautiful beaches on the Caspian Sea, but to go swimming I have to travel to Turkey. Because I can't talk to people here without fearing the consequences."

"You don't seem to be the kind of person who is easily intimidated."

"Most cops are younger than me. When they stop me on the street because of the loud music on my motorbike, I explain to them that they don't call the shots. I've never had serious problems with them."

Shyness is not in the nature of Iranians, though, as I realize the next morning in the 22 Bahman Primary School in the neighboring town of Salam Shahr. 22 Bahman is a date and stands for February 11, the anniversary of the revolution. Funman asked me whether I could give a short talk about the ecological aspects of my travels during a presentation about the handling of garbage. I selected a few photos and thought about a few clever phrases and am awaiting my turn from the first row in a large hall.

The national anthem blasts out of an Aiwa cassette player, and everyone stands up with their right hands on their hearts. The principal speaks, a teacher speaks, and a couple kids also speak and play some music on three keyboards. Finally, prizes are given to the winners of a painting competition, and there are cookies and grape juice from Tetra Paks. Funman wanders through the hall taking photos.

There doesn't seem to be time for my lecture, and it is spontaneously canceled. As compensation I'm allowed to participate in a lesson with the third class. The route from the hall to the classroom proves to be a real challenge because small boys in blue-black uniforms and skater sneakers continuously stop me and ask for my autograph, as if I were a pop star. I sign dozens of notepads and scraps of paper and answer questions about my country of origin, marital status, and soccer. An opportunity to clarify that Messi is better than Ronaldo, and that Borussia Dortmund is better than Bayern Munich.

In the classroom everyone individually introduces themselves in English. "Hello, my name is Farshad." "Hello, my name is Ahmad." "Hello, my name is Alireza."

It's oppressively hot in the classroom with no air conditioning. I feel a little like an exotic species, as I sit in front of the class telling of my travels so far, with Funman and their teacher translating into Persian. I only understand the place names. Kish, Kerman, Yazd, Shiraz, Isfahan, Mashhad. Finally, the teacher asks me if I have anything else that I would like to share with the kids.

"Learn English," I say, thinking of the *Animal Farm* book in the library. "And get to know your country, travel around. It's a wonderful country."

Through a jostling horde of schoolboys, I walk with Funman across the playground to the road, past two soccer goals and a wall brightly painted with a map of Iran. The noise is so deafening that even the two teachers running by fail to control it. After how many reprimands do children lose this wildness? Please preserve a bit of it; don't ever become apathetic—that is what I should have told them.

To: PeaceGulf Tehran
Hi Reza, how are you? I contacted you some weeks ago on cs. would it be possible that I stay at your place for 2 nights from thursday? would be great!

From: PeaceGulf Tehran
Sure Stephan you can stay with me

To: PeaceGulf Tehran
Wow, that was a quick reply:) thanks so much, see you soon!

From: PeaceGulf Tehran
:)

LIFE'S CARAVAN

IRANIANS LOVE THE northern area of their country because it is greener here than elsewhere, because there are swimming beaches, because of the rain and the mountains. If you travel west along the Caspian Sea, there is similar scenery for hundreds of miles: to the right, the sea, to the left forests, and towering above them, the peaks of mountains, some impressive and others not so. Kiwi plantations and rice paddies resembling those on the high plains of Vietnam. And the gray, landlocked sea, bordering on five different countries. If the world weren't curved, you could stand on any beach and have a panoramic view of Azerbaijan, Russia, Kazakhstan, and Turkmenistan. Apart from that, there isn't much to arouse the interest of Western visitors. We know similar landscapes from home and are more spellbound by deserts and architectural masterpieces.

I travel along the coast to Astara, near to the border with Azerbaijan, by bus, and then inland to Ardabil, where an MD-80 plane, vintage 1989, transports me back to Tehran. The Elburz

Mountains loom ahead, and all the gray cardboard-carton houses of Tehran, the cars in the daily traffic jams, and the Milad Tower. To the east I can make out Mount Damavand, the highest mountain in Iran, a nineteen-thousand-foot snow-capped pyramid clearly contrasted against the blue sky.

Its image hangs between dozens of other tourist posters and maps and handwritten poems in Reza's basement. Reza, forty, online name "PeaceGulf," is maybe the most experienced couchsurfing member in Iran. In five years he has collected 1,058 friends and 798 reviews. His reputation precedes him: a number of my hosts have already mentioned that he has been arrested twenty times, that he has argued with members of the government about couchsurfing, that he was the first in the country to offer accommodation, that he has room for fifty guests, and that he is clever and interesting, but nevertheless that staying overnight is not exactly a luxurious experience.

Reza greets me briefly at the door, a well-built man with large glasses, little hair, and white rubber sandals. "I'm in the middle of teaching. Just go downstairs and get to know the others!" A narrow staircase leads to the basement: someone is playing the accordion and singing in French. There are six guests here: one from Malaysia and five from France. The latter are traveling around the world in an old trailer and showing short film clips, with a screen and projector that they have with them. They call their project Nomadic Cinema. They've been to Poland, Serbia, and Turkey, and they plan on driving to Turkmenistan and Kazakhstan. They are not yet sure, however, whether they will be able to put on a performance in Iran. "Here we have to be very careful that a topic isn't too erotic," says Sophie, one of the cineasts.

251

The rooms are full of odds and ends, the largest room being dominated by a ping-pong table on which there is a laminated hand-drawn map showing nearby Internet cafés, food stores, and subway stations. The atmosphere is more like a backpacker hostel than a private apartment. In a small storeroom I discover a camp bed; otherwise, there are only a few cushions there. Without your own camping mats you have to sleep on the stone floor—a point that Reza makes absolutely clear in his profile.

Soon the host comes down, and we sit on garden chairs and chat about couchsurfing in Iran. "Until six months ago I could let guests stay at my parents' home," says Reza, who studied electrotechnology in Tehran and philosophy in Toronto. "My mother made strict rules: they had to leave the house by nine in the morning and not return before nine at night—to sleep. Now I have a whole floor for my guests; my parents live on the top floor."

I ask him about his job.

"I give private English lessons, but apart from that, I don't work much." He has plenty of time to organize meetings. A hell of a lot of meetings. Saturdays: Hafiz evening and poetry soiree; Sundays: Ferdowsi meeting; Mondays: recitals of Saadi Shirazi poems; Tuesdays: Reza cooks a vegetarian lunch using his own recipes and holds free English conversation lessons ("We talk about subjects that aren't usually raised, such as women's rights or Labor Day"); Wednesdays: Arabic; Thursdays: hiking and collecting litter in the north of Tehran; Fridays: Omar Khayyam poetry. And sometimes Reza takes foreign guests to a school for Afghani refugees or just plays ping-pong with a couple people.

I ask him whether he ever has problems with the authorities because of his many guests and meetings. "Once I was contacted by a couchsurfer from Israel. We had a lively exchange of posts, and I gave him a review. The staff at the Ministry of Tourism found this suspicious. They asked me what it was all about. Actually, they weren't against couchsurfing, rather they were trying to find a way to make this kind of tourism acceptable to the police. Our idea was to set up a website where the host could register the guest just like hotels do. Then no one would suspect us of concealing foreign spies." This hasn't been implemented yet. He has often been hauled in front of the police but is pretty relaxed about it. "I always explain that I like having foreign guests and that seems to be okay." His certificate as a tourist guide makes things easier. "In Tehran much worse things happen than couchsurfing. There are private orgies and illegal parties. The police are also considerably more interested in secret political events." I think of Atefeh in Kerman, whose guide license was revoked because she had foreign guests. There seem to be considerable regional differences as to which breaches of law are punished.

It's Friday, so in the evening I go with Reza to Laleh Park, to the Omar Khayyam event. Some fifteen people have come; many are students. Among them is the twenty-seven-year-old designer Setareh, who contacted me saying that she was interested in my travels because she also dreams of seeing more of her country. We sit in a kind of amphitheater, with people around playing volleyball or badminton. Doing the rounds, each gives a short account of himself or herself. One is an engineer who now studies sociology. Another is an Islamicist who now works in the theater. There is an artist who gave up 253 studying for his economics degree years ago. An author working on a book about deliverance from the cocoon of religious constraints. An agronomist who recently changed to study Western philosophy. And a programmer who would rather be a singer. Of course, he is immediately asked to give us a song, and with a mellow voice he sings an Omar Khayyam poem:

> Life's caravan is hastening on its way;
> Brood not on troubles of the coming day,
> But fill the wine-cup, ere sweet night be gone,
> And snatch a pleasant moment, while you may.[1]

"Bravo," says Reza; the rest clap. A crowd of people trying to follow their true passions, instead of fitting the norms. "That happens a lot," explains Reza. "Social pressure forces young people to pounce on a profession that doesn't really reflect their interests."

254   Setareh is on a slightly different path. She has a bachelor's degree in graphic design but now studies tourist management because the job prospects are better. After about two hours the introductory round is over, and we stroll a while to the

Khayyam statue, to read out some of his poems. The stone likeness of the poet and mathematician is leaning on a thick tome, a bottle of wine at his feet. Sternly, but not without benevolence, he looks down at us. It is truly wonderful to witness the enthusiasm of the students for the 1,900-year-old hedonistic poetry; the language sounds like music. I feel as if I've landed in a Persian version of *Dead Poets Society*.

"The big difference between Khayyam and the Islamic mystics was that the mystics were always thinking of the 'beyond,' while the poet was celebrating the 'here and now,'" says Reza. To put it another way: faced with a decision of whether to have a good wine in this life or seventy-two virgins a little later, Khayyam would always go for the drink.

From: Setareh
Hi, one of my friend is planning a party tomorrow around 5pm. Do you want to come?

To: Setareh
Hi setareh, sounds great, i d love to join you! see you tomorrow!

COUNTRY OF SURPRISES

NEXT MORNING I meet Setareh near Tehran's bazaar for a tour of the city. She takes me to Mr. Rezai's poster business, where she often worked. The diversity of motifs is immense: deer in the forest, alpine chalets, Jesus at the Last Supper, squiggly *Quran* verses, Khomeini at prayer, 3-D pictures of ayatollahs Khomeini and Khamenei, where, depending on the angle, you can see one or the other's head.

Setareh shows me a London picture, bright red double-decker buses against a black-and-white background. "I did that one," she says. Somehow the image seems very familiar. "Okay, I found the image on the Internet. It's an easy job and well paid." In Iran there are a multitude of very strict laws covering many aspects of life but not copyright. A couple stores farther on there are software programs costing hundreds of dollars in Europe, and here they virtually give them away. Photoshop for $2 and Microsoft Office for $1.50.

"I have a surprise for you," says Setareh at lunch in a small restaurant serving *gheymeh*, a delicious meat and lentil dish.

"What?"

"I've organized an interview for you. *Donya-e-Eqtesad*, one of the biggest dailies in the country, wants to do something on your travels."

"How did you manage that?"

"One of my profs has a contact there; it was easy. When will suit you?"

"Tomorrow afternoon?"

"Okay, I'll call them."

The thought of getting to know such a media concern from the inside appeals to me. Of course, I will have to leave out plenty of details so that the story can be printed. As she telephones I notice that my Persian has improved. I understand a number of words and courtesies. And the word *Spiegel*.

"Tomorrow afternoon's fine, at five," she says after hanging up.

"Did you tell them that I work for *Der Spiegel*?"

"Of course; they were very interested."

"Did you also tell them I'm writing a book about Iran?"

"Yes, was that wrong?"

"I don't know. Maybe the interview isn't such a good idea."

Before we go to the after-work party in the afternoon, two other strange things happen. On the street a man in his fifties suddenly shouts: "Stephan! *Salam!* How are you?" I recognize his face, but at first I can't place it. Then I remember. We met in the border town of Hajij, in the evening after our interrogation. Hajij is 260 miles away, and Tehran has a population of 10 million—an incredible coincidence.

Two hours later Setareh shows me a park, where we want to relax a bit. "Hardly any tourists come here," she claims. We sit on a bench and promptly see a couple on a blanket some 150 feet away who even from this distance look like foreigners.

"Look, tourists!" I say.

She seems seriously surprised. A few moments later there are some drops of rain, and the couple get up and walk toward us.

"Stephan?!" says one of them.

"Clemens?!" I reply. He is a travel blogger touring with his girlfriend, Annette. We know each other from Hamburg. Hamburg is 2,300 miles away, and Tehran has many parks—another incredible chance meeting. Their plane landed this morning, and they plan to explore Yazd, Shiraz, and Isfahan on a two-week vacation. A coincidence like that just has to be celebrated with a beer, so Setareh invites them to the party this afternoon. We buy a pack of candy as a present, and then she takes us up to an office on the fourth floor of a faceless office building. The company sells security cameras. Five cheerful people between twenty-three and thirty greet us with a poster in the colors of the German flag on which is printed *Welcome—Love Stephan Iran*—and with the music of Rammstein from an MP3 player.

I rather like the imperative implied in the lines. "Actually it should read *Dear Stephan, welcome to Iran*," explains Setareh, as I tell her of its meaning. "It's much nicer as it is," I insist.

Two of the people present work here. Now they have called it a day and invited a circle of friends to the office to drink some beer. On the table there are Cheetos and pretzel sticks, on the walls various display models of security cameras, which lend a slightly paranoid atmosphere to the proceedings. "Don't worry, they're not on," says Ashkan, amateur brewer and office worker, on observing my worried look. "Would you like beer or tea?"

His dark beer, served out of a Delster soft drink bottle, is excellent. "Quaffable and full of flavor," pronounces Annette, who on the basis of her place of birth is the best judge of hop juice of those present—she comes from Franconia. "Every month I make two hundred pints of the stuff. It is a bit stronger than normal beer, about 10 per cent," says Ashkan. Incidentally, the next party is tomorrow, at the house of Jafar, a bearded engineer who retrained as an architect. He plays piano and is a big fan of the bands Dream Theater and Porcupine Tree. We are all invited.

Suddenly there is a terrific crack, like a shot, and the sound of breaking glass falling to the floor. A windowpane is broken, and some of the slats of the blind are destroyed. For a moment, total silence. Ashkan inspects the damage. "The wind blew a tile from a neighboring roof through the pane," he says. It is now pretty drafty, so we move the chairs and drinks to an adjoining room. The women disappear to the kitchen and bring back a couple plates of pasta and tomato sauce.

Jafar, the architect, worked for five years for the defense ministry and knows all there is to know about spying and intelligence work. I ask him what he thinks about my forthcoming newspaper interview. "It could be dangerous for you," he replies. "And for us, as you are coming to us after the interview, and we are having a party. Somebody could follow you."

259

Oh yes, I had forgotten: rogue state. There it is again, the fear of getting into trouble with the authorities. I had managed to blank it out. It only came back for one day in Mashhad, when I was applying for my visa. The travel experiences, the happy-go-lucky days on the road, the normality of the daily life with exceptionally warm-hearted people make it easy to forget the dangers.

"You have no idea how professionally the secret services work here, better than in almost any other country in the world. They collect the data of tourists in hotels, bug telephones, and check text messages. Your interview is with one of the biggest newspapers, so a member of intelligence will definitely be listening in. Maybe, directly afterward, you will be invited to another interview. That is not an experience that I would wish on you. Think carefully about it."

"I don't think there's a lot to think about. I'm going to cancel it."

"That's very wise," says Jafar.

HAPPY ENDING

A GALLON OF RAISIN schnapps for ten guests may appear to be a bit extreme, but the dealer didn't want to sell smaller quantities. Additionally, there are two four-gallon plastic containers of Jafar's home brew beer in a storage room off his hall. Nobody's going to die of thirst. My flight to Hamburg is arranged for tomorrow, so this is a kind of leaving party.

A clear segregation of genders takes place between the front door and the living room. The men enter and head, more or less directly, for the schnapps container, and the women disappear to a side room for ten minutes to dispose of their headscarves and coats, only to reappear in spectacular dresses.

Jafar has an expensively decorated penthouse apartment, with a stone floor and a magnificent view of the Milad Tower in the evening light.

Dark gray clouds hang above the skyscrapers of Tehran, and on the horizon you can see the flashes of an approaching thunderstorm. From a rooftop on an adjacent building a man appears to be watching us. I quickly redraw the drapes.

A number of images of Jesus and crucifixes are arranged on tables and closets. "I am the only person in the clique who is religious," says Jafar. "But I'm a Christian, not a Muslim."

He sits at his Korg electric piano and improvises expertly on a rock song. He hands me an electric guitar, and soon we are all singing Adele and Guns N' Roses songs and a couple voluptuous-sounding Persian tunes. We drink and dance, men with men ("But we're not gay!"), women with men, women with women—a relaxed circle of friends. It would be easy to forget where we are if there weren't moments when a sudden melancholy mood descends on the gathering like a dark cloud.

Ashkan is here with his girlfriend, Nazanin. They have been together a couple years. He says that he dreams of being able, once in his life, to take her to a bar and order her a cocktail—in public, in front of everyone. "Is that too much to ask?" I notice that he is close to tears.

Shortly afterward, Jafar returns to the subject of surveillance. He suggests storing all my photos and text files on his computer. "Just in case they are confiscated at the airport. It would be even better if you trashed all photos of parties, military posts, and nuclear plants."

While I'm transferring forbidden and innocent pictures onto Jafar's computer, Setareh sits down next to me. "I want to show you something." She sets up a VPN connection to access blocked websites and types the search term "Happy Tehran" into YouTube. What you can see on the clip closely resembles what is happening in the living room behind us: six young people, three men and three women, are dancing happily to Pharrell Williams's upbeat hit, F minor, 160 bpm. On the staircase, in the living room, on the balcony with a view of the Milad Tower. Sometimes alone, sometimes man and woman together. Headgear includes hats and headbands but no veils or headscarves. The song's lyrics talk about freedom and ask you to join in clapping if you feel that happiness is the truth. These words are an invitation to seize the moment, similar to Omar Khayyam's: "But fill the wine-cup, ere sweet night be gone, and snatch a pleasant moment, while you may."[1] The poet understood it all nine hundred years ago. At the end of the video clip the names of the "happy" troupe are superimposed, in some cases with last names together with a short message: *Happy was an excuse to be happy. We enjoyed every second of making it. Hope it puts a smile on your face.*

This simple appeal didn't please all viewers. "They were all arrested," says Setareh. The police only took six hours from the beginning of their investigations until the arrests. They were accused of violating Islamic morals and customs, and they spent three days in prison. A few days ago, while I was touring northern Iran, they were freed on bail. Later they were sentenced to six months in prison and ninety-one lashes, albeit on probation. Tehran's chief of police, Hossein Sajedinia, used the publicity as a warning to Iran's youth, as if to say: "The police are alert and always ready to act against those of you not conforming to the social norms." The video was suddenly no longer available on YouTube. "Iran is a country where being 'happy' is a crime," tweeted the well-known journalist Golnaz Esfandiari.

Young people are in the majority. Forty-four million Iranians, 60 per cent of the total population, are under thirty. I have met only a few dozen of them. My travels are not a representative survey but encounters with a select group, a group who speaks English, is interested in travel and life in the West, and striving for more freedom. A group who has developed a remarkable routine of breaching laws despite the threat of

263

draconian punishment. Never in the thirty-five years of the Islamic Republic have there been so many of them.

Their social revolution takes place behind closed doors. And in the digital world. Flirting on Viber, putting their headscarves aside on Facebook, posting scandalous clips on YouTube. The Internet allows more freedom than reality does. It is still an escape from the public arena, but at some stage, testing the boundaries online will appeal so much that they can no longer accept being contained offline. "The change in Iran must come peacefully and from within,"[2] wrote the Nobel Peace Prize winner Shirin Ebadi.

I have the impression that the young Iranians haven't yet realized the power potential provided by sheer numbers and that they have a real chance to transform their country.

I go to the window. Behind me the party is in full swing, but I block it out for a short while just to observe the cardboard-box skyline of the city. Tens of thousands of apartment blocks, with shuttered windows and locked doors, visual barriers behind which the craziest and most normal things in the world take place every day. Maybe somewhere a flight dispatcher plays *Flight Simulator*, a dominatrix binds her slaves, a graphic design teacher visits friends for an evening meal, a fishing boat owner sings a melancholic song, an engineer hops around in the kitchen trying to catch a bird, a war vet plays backgammon, a prince treats himself to another glass of wine, a nature boy sorts saffron blossoms, a pretty student has a date in the living room, a truck driver listens to Modern Talking, an English teacher types into his computer the invitations to the next Dead Poets Society meeting.

Midday tomorrow I will board a plane. TK875 to Istanbul, back to the future, 621 years forward. I will show my German passport, check my backpack, and drink my last bottle of Delster. Then I'm out, back to a world where no one has to be afraid of being arrested for a trifle, where no one is forced to follow a particular religion, where normality isn't a game of hide-and-seek.

On the plane I will have a hangover from the schnapps and the catchy melody of "Happy" buzzing around in my head. The Tehran video clip was only briefly offline; now it is again accessible. More than 2 million people all round the world have already seen it, and the number increases every day. No one can sentence the dancers a second time.

They have won.

"Happy" video

ACKNOWLEDGMENTS

I WOULD LIKE TO warmly thank the following people, without whom this book would not have been possible: Yasmin in Tehran, Masoud on Kish, Hussein in Kerman, Saeed in Shiraz, Ahmad in Bushehr, Marjan in Bushehr, Farshad in Ahvaz, Hamed and Ashkan in Khorramabad, Azim and Susan in Kermanshah, Ehsan in Marivan, Shahin and Mona in Hamedan, Ahmad in Isfahan, Sofia in Isfahan, Mellid in Isfahan, Massi in Isfahan, Elaheh in Mashhad, Azadeh in Babol, Saeed in Chalus, Funman Mohamed in Abbas Abad, Azim and Nilo in Choubar, Hussein in Ardabil, Reza in Tehran, Shahab in Tehran, Venus in Tehran, Kian on Qeshm, Setareh in Tehran, Fardad, Hamed, Babak, Sahar, Mina, Arash, Negar, Anita, Maryam, Ali, Mohsen, Abbas, Marzieh, Helaleh, Narjes, Pedram, Sahar and Nazanin, Laila, Anastasiya Izhak, Rüdiger Ditz, Mina Esfandiari (minaesfandiari.com), Martina Klüver, Bettina Feldweg, Jule Fischer, Samuel Zuder (samuelzuder.com), Marina and Yiannis of Marili Apartments on Paros (marili-studios.gr), Nora Reinhardt, Katrin Schmiedekampf, Stefan Schultz, Azadeh F. Parsi,

Verena Töpper, Anja Tiedge, Nasser Manouchehri, Marouso Triantafyllou, Aysegül Eraslan, Ben Wadewitz, Annette Schneider, Clemens Sehi (anekdotique.de), Johannes Klaus (reisedepeschen.de), the Goethe-Institut, Antje Blinda, Lena Hinz, Kitty Liu, Tom Hillenbrand, Philip Laubach-Kiani, Astrid Därr, Anja Lange, Tonia Sorrentino, Bianca Bontempo, Mareike Engelken, Melanie Maier, Anouk Joester, Janine Borse, Hallie Gu, Christian Byfield, my parents.

Couchsurfing in Iran: My Journeys Behind Closed Doors on Facebook: www.facebook.com/couchsurfingimiran and on Instagram: couchsurfingiranwww.travelepisodes.com/reise/couchsurfing-im-iran/

NOTES

At the border

1. Satrapi, Marjane. *Persepolis: The Story of a Childhood.* New York: Pantheon Books, 2003.

Torture

1. James, E.L. *Fifty Shades of Grey.* New York: Vintage Books, 2012.

The Persian Gulf

1. Hill, Napoleon. *Think and Grow Rich.* New York: Jeremy P. Tarcher/Penguin, 2011.

2. Covey, Stephen R. *The 7 Habits of Highly Effective People: Powerful Lessons in Personal Change.* New York: Simon & Schuster, 1989.

3. Robbins, Anthony. *Awaken the Giant Within: How to Take Immediate Control of Your Mental, Emotional, Physical and Financial Destiny!* New York: Summit Books, 1991.

Hide-and-seek

1. Browne, Edward Granville. *A Year Amongst the Persians: Impressions as to the Life, Character & Thought of the People of Persia, Received During Twelve Months' Residence in that Country in the Years 1887–1888.* New York: Cambridge University Press, 1926, p. 240.

Notes

Poetry

1. Hafiz. *Poems from the Divan of Hafiz.* Translated by Gertrude Bell. London: William Heinemann, 1897, p. 72.

2. Ibid., p. III.

3. Ibid., p. 104.

4. Ibid., p. 67.

5. Goethe, Johann Wolfgang von. *Goethe's Faust.* Parts I and II. Translated by Louis MacNeice. New York: Oxford University Press, 1952.

6. Celan, Paul. "Death Fugue." *70 Poems.* Translated by Michael Hamburger. New York: Persea Books Inc., 2013.

Hiking

1. Hafiz. *Poems from the Divan of Hafiz.* Translated by Gertrude Bell. London: William Heinemann, 1897, p. 103.

Life's caravan

1. Khayyam, Omar. *The Quatrains of Omar Khayyam.* Second edition. Translated by E.H. Whinfield. London: Kegan Paul, Trench, Trübner, & Co. Ltd., 1893, p. 51.

Happy ending

1. Khayyam, Omar. *The Quatrains of Omar Khayyam.* Second edition. Translated by E.H. Whinfield. London: Kegan Paul, Tranch, Trübner, & Co. Ltd., 1893, p. 51.

2. Ebadi, Shirin. *Iran Awakening: A Memoir of Revolution and Hope.* New York: Random House, 2006, p. 204.